POWER SYSTEM ENGINEERING

POWER SYSTEM ENGINEERING

C.M. ARORA
B.E. (Honours) Electrical Engg.,
AMIE (Electronics and Communication Engg.),
M.E. (Honours) Electrical Engg.,
Ph.D. (Electrical Engg.), FIE, LMISTE

Professor,
Dept. of Electrical Engineering,
Malaviya Regional Engineering College,
Jaipur.

GALGOTIA
Publications Pvt. Ltd.
5, Ansari Road, Darya Ganj, New Delhi-110 002

Galgotia Publications pvt. ltd.

First Edition - 2000

Reprint: 2013

ISBN 81-7515-326-1

Published by **Galgotia Publications Pvt. Ltd.,**
5, Ansari Road, Darya Ganj, New Delhi-110 002 and printed at
Earam Offset Printers, Delhi-110053

Galgotia Publications pvt. ltd.

To
My Mother Krishna Pyari Arora, Retd. Teacher
Wife Veena Arora
Daughter Sonal and
Son Atul

ABOUT THE AUTHOR

Dr. C. M. Arora is Professor in the Department of Electrical Engineering at Malaviya Regional Engineering College, Jaipur. He obtained his BE (Honours), ME (Honours) and Ph.D. from University of Jodhpur, Jodhpur. He has been a meritorious student and secured first position in ME with 89.5% marks and second position in BE with 72.4% marks. He has also received several first and second prizes for working models exhibited in district and school level science fairs.

Dr. Arora is a member of executive committee of Rajasthan Energy Development Agency (REDA). He is also the Chief Coordinator of an AICTE sponsored research project. He is a fellow of the Institution of Engineers (India) and life member of ISTE.

Professor Arora has also taught at MBM Engineering College, University of Jodhpur, Jodhpur from 1983-90. During this period he has taught to undergraduate as well as postgraduate classes in the area of Power System. His industrial experience has been with the Rajasthan State Electricity Board, Jaipur from 1978-1983 as Assistant Engineer. During this period he was engaged in the Analysis and Design of Power System.

Dr. Arora has been involved in the development of High Voltage Laboratory under AICTE Modernisation project at MBM Engineering College, University of Jodhpur, Jodhpur from Project Report preparation to implementation. He has been Co-coordinator of Science Centre at University of Jodhpur. He has also prepared a Project Report for Modernisation of Power System Laboratory at Malaviya Regional Engineering College, Jaipur which received grants from AICTE. He has been involved in the development of Power System Laboratory at MBM Engineering College, Jodhpur and at Malaviya Regional Engineering College, Jaipur.

Dr. Arora has delivered several expert lectures in a number of Winter and Summer schools to the teachers of Engineering Colleges and Universities and Engineers of Electrical utilities. He has also attended several national and international conferences.

Professor Arora is the author of numerous papers in various national and international journals and conferences. He received the Union Ministry of Irrigation and Power Prize 1993-94 for his paper entitled "A Direct Reconfiguration Algorithm for Minimising Losses in Radial Electric Distribution Systems".

PREFACE

"Power System Engineering" has been written primarily for the undergraduate students in Electrical Engineering. The book covers topics which are commonly taught in final year and at this stage the students have enough background knowledge of Power System. Therefore introductory part has been eliminated in this book to avoid repetition. The book has been written keeping in view the average and below average students but at the same time it is useful for improving understanding and score of above average students too.

The author is teaching the course from last many years and looking to the difficulties of his students in the classroom and examination, lecture notes have been prepared. The present book is outcome of these lecture notes. It also includes the research work carried by the author relevant to present needs. The author also has field experience as Assistant Engineer in Rajasthan State Electricity Board for five years and the book also incorporates his experiences with power system.

The material presented in the book has been tested in classroom and examination and it has been found that the material is very useful to the students for understanding as well as from examination point of view. Actually the students suggested and forced the author to write the book for greater benefits to all. The book is also useful to the teachers teaching this course.

The author has been a meritorious student obtaining second position in merit in B.E. (72.4% marks) and highest record marks in M.E. (89.5% marks). The author has made every effort in preparation of the material presented in the book such that the students using the book also acquire the quality comparable to the meritorious students.

I would like to acknowledge with gratitude the contributions of many individuals in the preparation of this book. I would also like to acknowledge the understanding and patience of my wife Veena and children Sonal and Atul during the preparation of the book.

The author will welcome suggestions for the improvement of the book.

C. M. ARORA

7th July, 2000

CONTENTS

Chapter 1 POWER SYSTEM ECONOMICS **1**

1.1 Reserve Capacity of Stations 1

1.1.1 Cold Reserve 1

1.1.2 Operating Reserve 1

1.2 Interconnection of Stations 2

1.3 Economic Loading 3

1.4 Input-output Curves 3

1.5 Incremental Rate Curves 4

1.6 Optimal Generation Scheduling (Transmission Losses Neglected) 6

1.7 Optimal Unit Commitment 11

1.8 Optimal Unit Commitment Using Dynamic Programming Method 11

1.9 Optimal Generation Scheduling (Including Transmission Losses) 18

1.10 Transmission Loss Formula 20

Review Questions 26

Chapter 2 ELEMENTS OF LOAD FREQUENCY CONTROL **27**

2.1 Flat Frequency Control 28

2.2 Flat Tie-line Load Control 28

2.3 Tie-line Load Bias Control 29

2.4 Governor Control 30

Review Questions 36

Chapter 3 VOLTAGE CONTROL **37**

3.1 Methods of Voltage Control 37

	3.2	Tap Changing Transformers	40
	3.3	On-load Tap Changer	44
	3.4	Shunt Capacitors and Reactors	45
	3.5	Series Capacitors	48
	3.6	Thyristorised Static Var Compensators	49
		3.6.1 Thyristor Controlled Reactor (TCR)-Fixed Capacitor (FC) Compensator	49
		3.6.2 Thyristor Controlled Transformer (TCT) compensator	50
		3.6.3 Thyristor Switched Capacitor (TSC)-Thyristor Controlled Reactor (TCR) compensator	51
		3.6.4 Mechanically Switched Capacitor (MSC)-Thyristor Controlled Reactor (TCR) compensator	52
	3.7	Phase Angle Control	52
	3.8	Phase Shifting Transformers	53
	Review Questions		54
Chapter 4	**EXCITATION SYSTEMS**		**57**
	4.1	D.C. Excitation System	57
	4.2	A.C. Excitation System	58
		4.2.1 Rotating Thyristor Excitation System (Self Excited System)	59
		4.2.2 Brushless Excitation System (Separately Excited System)	60
	4.3	Automatic Voltage Regulators	61
		4.3.1 Rotary Amplifier or Servo Type (Use of Amplidyne) Automatic Voltage Regulator	62
		4.3.2 Magnetic Amplifier Type (Use of Magnetic Amplifier) Automatic Voltage Regulator	63
		4.3.3 Solid State (Electronic) type Automatic Voltage Regulator	65
	Review Questions		65

Chapter 5	**POWER SYSTEM STABILITY AND SECURITY**		**67**
	5.1	Meaning of Power System Stability	67
	5.2	Steady State, Transient and Dynamic Stability	68
		5.2.1 Steady State Stability	68
		5.2.2 Transient Stability	68
		5.2.3 Dynamic Stability	69
	5.3	Power Limits of Transmission Lines	70
		5.3.1 Steady State Stability Limit of a Transmission Line	70
		5.3.2 Transient Stability Limit of a Transmission Line	73
	5.4	Representation of Synchronous Machines	74
	5.5	Inertia Constant	82
	5.6	Swing Equation	85
	5.7	Equal Area Criterion	89
	5.8	Applications of Equal Area Criterion	93
		5.8.1 Sustained Line Fault	96
		5.8.2 Line Fault with Subsequent Clearing	98
		5.8.3 Line Fault with Subsequent Clearing Followed by Reclosing	99
	5.9	Application of Equal Area Criterion for two Finite Machines Case	117
	5.10	Factors Affecting Stability	119
		5.10.1 Steady State Stability	119
		5.10.2 Transient Stability Limit	119
	5.11	Power System Security	121
	Review Questions		123
Chapter 6	**EXTRA HIGH VOLTAGE TRANSMISSION**		**125**
	6.1	Need for Extra High Voltage (EHV) Transmission	125
	6.2	Surge Impedance Loading	127
	6.3	Electrostatic Fields of EHV Lines	127
	6.4	Corona Effect	129
	6.5	Corona Loss	130

6.6 Radio Noise from EHV Lines 131
6.7 Use of Bundled Conductors 133
6.8 Tuned Power Lines 134
6.8.1 Principle of Tuned Power Lines 134
6.8.2 Practical Considerations 136
6.8.3 Tuning of Transmission Lines 136
Review Questions 137

Chpater 7 HVDC TRANSMISSION 139
7.1 Types of DC Links 139
7.1.1 Monopolar Link 139
7.1.2 Bipolar Link 140
7.1.3 Homopolar Link 141
7.2 Advantages of HVDC Transmission 141
7.3 Disadvantages of HVDC Transmission 143
7.4 Converter Station Equipment 144
7.4.1 Converter Transformers 145
7.4.2 Filters 146
7.4.3 Reactive Power Source 146
7.4.4 Smoothing Reactors 146
7.4.5 DC Switchgear 146
7.5 Ground Return 146
7.6 Applications 147
7.6.1 Power Transmission over Long Overhead Lines 147
7.6.2 Power Transmission through Underground or Submarine Cables 148
7.6.3 Interconnection of Individually Controlled AC Systems 148
7.6.4 AC and DC lines in Parallel 148
7.6.5 DC Transmission and AC Distribution 148
7.6.6 Interconnection of Different Frequency AC Systems 148
Review Questions 148

Chapter 1

POWER SYSTEM ECONOMICS

This chapter is aimed at the cost of generation of electrical energy in power systems. The cost of generation depends on the capital cost and the operating cost. These costs are highly influenced by the reserve capacity of stations, interconnection of stations, generator units in operation, and load-sharing among the operating units.

1.1 RESERVE CAPACITY OF STATIONS

Every generating station must have a certain amount of reserve capacity to facilitate periodic maintenance and repairs of its generating units and to meet demand of energy when a unit has a forced outage (due to fault etc.). A reserve generating capacity is also required to meet the minute to minute variation in load and the load forecasting errors. The reserve generating capacity may be classified into two categories as cold reserve and operating reserve.

1.1.1 Cold Reserve

The cold reserve is that reserve generating capacity which is available for service but is not in operation. It is used when a generating unit is to be taken out for maintenance or repair.

1.1.2 Operating Reserve

The operating reserve is the reserve capacity above firm system load requirement to provide for minute to minute variation in load, load forecasting errors and forced outage of the units. It is of two types : hot reserve and spinning reserve.

(*a*) **Hot reserve** : It is that operating reserve capacity which is in operation but not in service. It is provided to meet the load demand under forced outage conditions.

(*b*) **Spinning reserve :** It is that operating reserve generating capacity which is connected to the system bus and is ready to take load. It is provided to meet minute to minute load variations and any extra load due to load forecasting errors.

1.2 INTERCONNECTION OF STATIONS

In an isolated generating station the practice is to provide reserve generating capacity as a generator equal to the largest size in the station to facilitate maintenance and repairs and to meet demand of energy when a unit has a forced outage. If every generating station works in isolation the total reserve capacity requirement of all stations, which is normally (or for most of the time) lying idle, would amount to considerable capacity. The total reserve capacity can be considerably reduced if the generating stations are interconnected. In the interconnected system the reserve capacity required is equal to the largest size of the generator unit in the system. Under conditions of outage of a generating unit it is immediately possible to borrow power from adjoining interconnected generating stations wherever reserve capacity is available. The interconnection of generating stations results in following advantages :

(*i*) On account of less reserve capacity required against outage of a unit, the total installed capacity needed for the whole system reduces. This saves much capital cost.

(*ii*) When generating stations are operated in isolation, each has to maintain separate spinning reserve capacity. When they are interconnected it may be sufficient to have a smaller total spinning reserve for the system for the same degree of reliability.

(*iii*) In an interconnected system it is possible to have larger generator ratings because excess capacity of a station may be utilized by the areas fed by other stations. As the size of a generator increases the capital cost per kW reduces. Therefore a saving is achieved in total capital cost.

(*iv*) On account of maximum demands of individual stations not occurring simultaneously, the maximum demand of combined or interconnected system is less than the sum of the individual maximum demands. Therefore total installed capacity required in interconnected system is lesser resulting in saving in capital cost.

(*v*) In the event of failure of a generating station to supply power, due to outage of its units or outage of transmission lines, the other generating stations can supply the surplus power available with them. Thus system interconnection leads to increase in reliability of electric supply.

(*vi*) The efficiency of all the generating stations is not equal. Some generating stations are more efficient and the others are less efficient. When the generating stations are interconnected, it is possible to shift load from less efficient generating stations to more efficient stations such that total operating cost is minimum. Therefore an interconnected system has less operating cost if the total load is shared by the generating stations according to economic loading of the stations.

The interconnection of generating stations results in following disadvantages :

(*i*) Interconnection of generating station involves expenses for construction of interconnecting transmission lines between generating stations or areas. These lines are called tie lines.

(*ii*) Interconnection causes larger currents to flow on transmission lines under faulty condition with a consequent increase in capacity of circuit breakers. Therefore expensive circuit breakers are required with interconnected system.

(*iii*) The generators of all the interconnected generating stations must operate at the same frequency and in a synchronised manner.

1.3 ECONOMIC LOADING

At a generating station the station load can be met by the generating units in many ways with different set of loadings on the units. Similarly, in an interconnected system the system load demand can be met by the generating stations in many ways with different set of loadings on the stations. The best choice out of these loadings is the loading of the generating stations/units which results in minimum total operating cost. The loading of the generating stations/units which results in minimum total operating cost is called economic loading of the generating stations/units.

The major component of the operating cost is the cost of fuel input per hour while maintenance contributes only to a small extent which may be neglected or taken as a small proportion of fuel cost. Therefore the fuel input versus power output characteristic, also known as input-output curves, of generating units/stations are only considered for determining the economic loading of the generating stations/units. The input-output curves and its derivative, called incremental rate curves, are defined as follows :

1.4 INPUT-OUTPUT CURVES

The graphical relation between the fuel input (in Rs. per hour or million kilocalories per hour) and power output (in kW or MW) for any generating unit or generating station is known as input-output curve. A typical input-output curve is shown in Fig. 1.1.

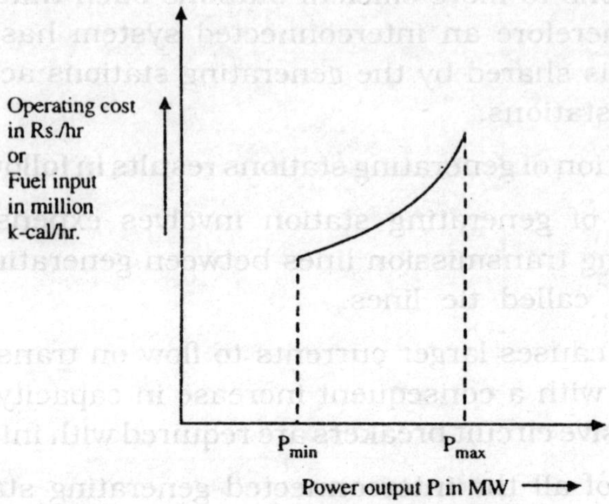

Fig. 1.1 : A typical input-output curve

The P_{min} is the minimum loading limit below which it is uneconomical or technically infeasible to operate the unit or station and P_{max} is maximum output limit due to its rating.

The analytical expression for operating cost in Rs./hr or input in million K-cal/hr can be written as

$$C(P) = \alpha + \beta P + \Gamma P^2 + \ldots \text{ Rs./hr or million k-cal/hr}$$

Generally it is sufficient to fit a second degree polynomial. There may be a number of units (stations) in a power station (system). For each unit (station) an expression for operating cost in Rs./hr or million k-cal/hr can be obtained as

$$C_i(P_i) = \frac{1}{2} a_i P_i^2 + b_i P_i + d_i \quad \text{Rs./hr or million k-cal/hr} \quad \ldots(1.1)$$

where suffix i stands for the unit/station number. The expression is true for $P_{i,\,min} < P_i < P_{i,\,max}$.

1.5 INCREMENTAL RATE CURVES

The graphical relation between the slope of input-output curve and power output for any generating unit/station is known as incremental rate curve. A typical incremental rate curve is shown in Fig. 1.2.

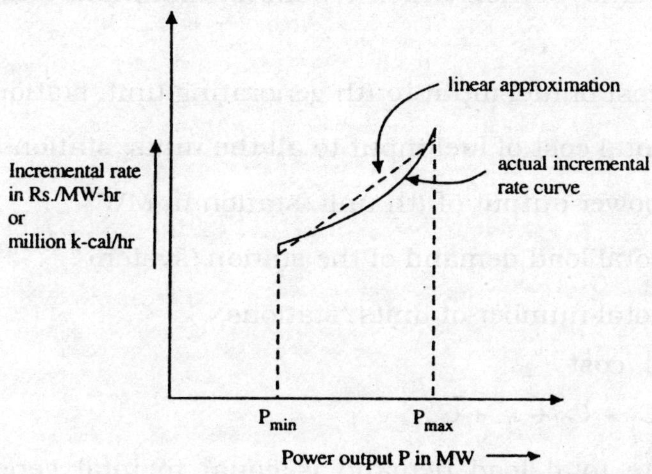

Fig. 1.2 : A typical incremental rate curve

The mathematical expression of the incremental rate curve is the incremental rate of the unit/station, which can be obtained as first derivative of the input-output function with respect to the output. Therefore if the input-output curve is expressed as

$$C_i(P_i) = \frac{1}{2} a_i P_i^2 + b_i P_i + d_i$$

then incremental rate IC_i is given by

$$IC_i = \frac{dC_i}{dP_i} = a_i P_i + b_i \text{ million k-cal/MW-hr or Rs./MW-hr} \quad ..(1.2)$$

Incremental rate may also be defined as the ratio of incremental input (increase in input) to the incremental output (increase in output) or

$$\text{Incremental rate} = \frac{\text{incremental input}}{\text{incremental output}} = \frac{\Delta C_i}{\Delta P_i}$$

Incremental rate is usually expressed in million k-cal/MW-hr. If it is expressed in Rs./MW-hr then it is usually called as incremental cost. However, the incremental rate and incremental cost are usually interchangeably used.

1.6 OPTIMAL GENERATION SCHEDULING (TRANSMISSION LOSSES NEGLECTED)

The optimal generation scheduling problem is the problem of determining output of each generating unit/station which results in minimum total operating cost.

Let :

C_i = cost of fuel input to ith generating unit/station in Rs./hr

C_t = total cost of fuel input to all the units/stations in Rs./hr

P_i = power output of ith unit/station in MW

P_D = total load demand of the station/system

n = total number of units/stations.

The total fuel cost

$$C_t = C_1 + C_2 + \dots + C_n \quad \text{...(1.3)}$$

In steady state total load demand is equal to total generation therefore

$$P_D = P_1 + P_2 + \dots + P_n = \sum_{i=1}^{n} P_i \quad \text{...(1.4)}$$

It is required to calculate P_i, $i = 1, 2, \dots, n$ which result in minimum total cost C_t and also satisfy Eq. (1.4). The problem is constrained optimization problem. The optimization problem can be solved by the method of Lagrange multipliers, which is used for minimizing (or maximizing) a function with the condition in the form of equality constraints. Using this method an augmented cost function (Lagrangian) is defined as

$$\overline{C}_t = C_t - \lambda \left(\sum_{i=1}^{n} P_i - P_D \right) \quad \text{...(1.5)}$$

where λ is the Lagrange multiplier.

The minimization is achieved under the condition

$$\frac{\partial \overline{C}_t}{\partial P_i} = 0$$

or $$\frac{\partial C_t}{\partial P_i} - \lambda = 0$$

or $$\frac{\partial C_t}{\partial P_i} = \lambda \qquad ...(1.6)$$

Since the cost of fuel input to ith unit C_i depends on the output of that unit P_i only therefore using Eq. (1.3)

$$\frac{\partial C_t}{\partial P_i} = \frac{dC_i}{dP_i} \text{ for } i = 1, 2, ..., n \qquad ...(1.7)$$

from Eqs. (1.6) and (1.7)

$$\frac{dC_1}{dP_1} = \frac{dC_2}{dP_2} = ... = \frac{dC_n}{dP_n} = \lambda \qquad ...(1.8)$$

or $$IC_1 = IC_2 = ... = IC_n = \lambda \qquad ...(1.9)$$

Thus optimal operation is achieved if every unit operates at the same incremental cost. This criterion is called as equal incremental cost criterion. Optimum generation scheduling can be obtained by solving Eqs. (1.8) and (1.4). The Eq. (1.8) is called coordination equation.

The graphical solution of Eqs. (1.4) and (1.8) is illustrated by the graph shown in Fig. 1.3 for a two unit system for which it is required to satisfy the condition

$$P_D = P_1 + P_2 \qquad ...(1.10)$$

where P_D is the total load demand.

In the graph shown in Fig. 1.3 the horizontal line AB is shifted parallel to itself such that its intersection with the incremental cost characteristics representing P_1 and P_2 satisfy the Eq. (1.10). The horizontal line AB represents equal incremental cost line. The values of P_i thus obtained are the optimum generator outputs.

The analytical numerical solution is possible by first assuming certain value of λ, calculating values of P_i, $i = 1, 2, ..., n$ from Eq. (1.8) for this λ and comparing their sum ΣP_i with P_D. If ΣP_i is more than P_D then value of λ is decreased by $\Delta\lambda$ (a suitable step size), and if ΣP_i is less than P_D then value of λ is increased by $\Delta\lambda$. With the new value of λ the process is repeated till deviations in ΣP_i from P_D is less than a prescribed limit or deviations in P_i in subsequent repetitions is less than prescribed tolerance.

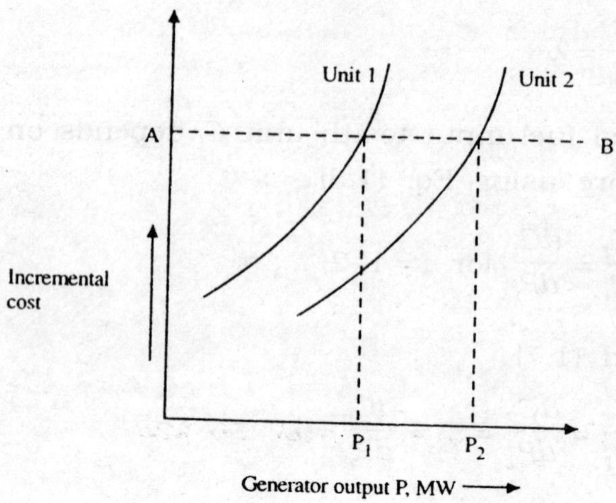

Fig. 1.3 : Graphical solution for obtaining optimal outputs

If $\frac{dC_i}{dP_i}$ is expressed by Eq. (1.2) then the analytical solution is obtained by a very simple method as follows. From Eqs. (1.2) and (1.8) one can write

$$P_i = \frac{\lambda - b_i}{a_i} \quad \text{...(1.11)}$$

therefore, $\Sigma P_i = \Sigma \frac{\lambda - b_i}{a_i}$

using Eq. (1.4) it becomes

$$\Sigma \frac{\lambda - b_i}{a_i} = P_D \quad \text{...(1.12)}$$

Given the value of P_D, the value of λ can be calculated using Eq. (1.12). Knowing the value of λ the optimum values of P_i, $i = 1, 2, ..., n$ can be calculated using Eq. (1.11).

The limits on generator output, $P_{i, max}$ and $P_{i, min}$, are taken in account as follows. If a particular generator loading P_i violates the limit $P_{i, max}$ or $P_{i, min}$, its loading is held fixed at the limit violated and the balance load is then shared among the remaining generators on equal incremental cost basis. The process is repeated till all the generator outputs are within limits.

Example 1.1. The incremental costs in Rs. per MW-hour of two 250 MW units are as under :

$$\frac{dC_1}{dP_1} = 0.20P_1 + 30 \quad ...(1.13)$$

$$\frac{dC_2}{dP_2} = 0.15P_2 + 40 \quad ...(1.14)$$

The minimum load of each is 20 MW. Find the economic loading of each of the two units for a total load of

(*a*) 225 MW, and (*b*) 50 MW.

Solution : The economic loading is achieved when

$$\frac{dC_1}{dP_1} = \frac{dC_2}{dP_2} \quad ...(1.15)$$

using Eqs. (1.13), (1.14) and (1.15) for economic loading

$$0.20P_1 + 30 = 0.15P_2 + 40$$

or $$P_1 = 0.75P_2 + 50 \quad ...(1.16)$$

(*a*) For a total load of 225 MW

For a total load of 225 MW the sum of the generator outputs

$$P_1 + P_2 = 225 \quad ...(1.17)$$

From Eqs. (1.16) and (1.17)

$$0.75P_2 + 50 + P_2 = 225$$

or $$1.75P_2 = 175$$

or $$P_2 = 100 \text{ MW} \quad ...(1.18)$$

Now from Eqs. (1.17) and (1.18)

$$P_1 = 225 - P_2 = 225 - 100 = 125 \text{ MW} \quad ...(1.19)$$

Thus for a total load of 225 MW the economic loadings of the units are $P_1 = 125$ MW and $P_2 = 100$ MW.

(*b*) For a total load of 50 MW

For a total load of 50 MW the sum of the generator outputs

$$P_1 + P_2 = 50 \quad ...(1.20)$$

From Eqs. (1.16) and (1.20)

$$0.75P_2 + 50 + P_2 = 50$$

or $$1.75P_2 = 0$$

or $$P_2 = 0 \text{ MW} \quad ...(1.21)$$

Since minimum load of each unit is 20 MW therefore P_2 is taken as 20 MW and remaining load (50 – 20) = 30 MW is met by the first unit and so $P_1 = 30$ MW.

Example 1.2. For the units of Example 1.1, calculate the saving per year for economic loading compared to equal load division between the units when the total load is 225 MW throughout the year.

Solution : The Eqs. (1.13) and (1.14) can be written as

$$dC_1 = (0.20P_1 + 30)\, dP_1 \quad ...(1.22)$$

$$dC_2 = (0.15P_2 + 40)\, dP_2 \quad ...(1.23)$$

Integrating these equations the operating cost of the units can be obtained as

$$C_1 = 0.100P_1^2 + 30P_1 + k_1 \quad ...(1.24)$$

$$C_2 = 0.075P_2^2 + 40P_2 + k_2 \quad ...(1.25)$$

where k_1 and k_2 are constants.

The total operating cost C_t is given by

$$C_t = C_1 + C_2$$

or $$C_t = 0.100P_1^2 + 30P_1 + k_1 + 0.075P_2^2 + 40P_2 + k_2 \quad ...(1.26)$$

For equal load division between the two units

$$P_1 = 112.5 \text{ MW and } P_2 = 112.5 \text{ MW},$$

giving total operating cost

C_t (equal loading)

$$= 0.100\,(112.5)^2 + 30\,(112.5) + k_1 + 0.075\,(112.5)^2 + 40\,(112.5) + k_2$$

$$= 10089.843 + k_1 + k_2 \text{ Rs./hr}$$

From Example 1.1, for economic loading

$P_1 = 125$ MW and $P_2 = 100$ MW,

giving total operating cost

C_t (optimal loading)

$$= 0.100\,(125)^2 + 30\,(125) + k_1 + 0.075\,(100)^2 + 40\,(100) + k_2$$

$$= 10062.5 + k_1 + k_2 \text{ Rs./hr}$$

Therefore saving per year

$$= (10089.843 + k_1 + k_2) - (10062.5 + k_1 + k_2) \text{ Rs. per hr}$$

$$= 27.343 \text{ Rs. per hr.} = 27.343 \times 8760 \text{ Rs. per year}$$

$$= 239524.68 \text{ Rs. per year.}$$

1.7 OPTIMAL UNIT COMMITMENT

It is not economical to run all the units available all the time. The unit commitment deals with the problem of determining the units of a generating station that should operate for a particular load to minimize operating cost. The unit commitment problem is applicable for thermal power plants only because for other types of generating plants, such as hydro, the operating cost and start-up times are negligible therefore their on-off status is not important.

A simple but inaccurate method to solve the unit commitment problem is to assign priority for the generating units such that the most efficient unit is loaded first to be followed by the most efficient unit from the remaining units as the load increases.

Another method to solve the problem is to compute the most economical operating cost for all the possible combinations of the units and then select that combination which has the least operating cost among these. This method is highly time consuming. Considerable computational savings can be achieved by using some optimization techniques such as branch and bounce or a dynamic programming method for reaching to minimum operating cost combination as certain combinations need not be tried at all in these methods.

1.8 OPTIMAL UNIT COMMITMENT USING DYNAMIC PROGRAMMING METHOD

In practice, the unit commitment problem is solved for the complete load cycle. The total number of units available, their individual operating cost characteristics and the load cycle on the generating station are assumed to be known in advance. Further, it is assumed that the load on each unit or combination of units changes in suitably small but uniform step of size ΔP_D MW (e.g. 1 MW).

Let a cost function $F_N(x)$ be defined as follows :

$F_N(x)$ = the minimum cost in Rs./hr of generating x MW by N units

$f_N(y)$ = cost of generating y MW by the Nth unit (known in advance)

$F_{N-1}(x-y)$ = the minimum cost of generating $(x-y)$ MW by the remaining $(N-1)$ units.

[for $N=2$, $F_{2-1}(x-y) = F_1(x-y) = f_1(x-y)$ known in advance).

The application of dynamic programming results in the following recursive relation :

$$F_N(x) = \min_{y} \{f_N(y) + F_{N-1}(x-y)\} \qquad \text{...(1.27)}$$

Here value of y is varied from minimum load level to the maximum load level in the discrete steps of ΔP_D giving a set of values of the expression $[f_N(y) + F_{N-1}(x-y)]$. The minimum of these values is the optimum value of $F_N(x)$.

Using the recursive relation given by Eq. (1.27) one can easily determine the combination of units which requires minimum operating costs for load ranging in convenient steps from the minimum permissible load of the smallest unit to the sum of the capacities of all the available units. In this process the total minimum operating cost and the load shared by each unit of the optimal combination are automatically determined for each load level. The detailed procedure is as follows, which is also illustrated by Example 1.3.

Starting arbitrarily with any two units, the most economical combination is determined for all the discrete station load levels using Eq. (1.27) where for $N=2$, $F_{N-1}(x-y) = F_1(x-y) = f_1(x-y)$ which is known. At each station load level the most economic solution may be to run either unit or both units with a certain load sharing between the two. It may also be possible that all the combinations considered are infeasible for certain load levels. The most economical cost curve in discrete form for the two units thus obtained, can be viewed as the cost curve of a single equivalent unit. The third unit is now added and the procedure is repeated to find the cost curve of the three combined units considering first two units as single equivalent unit. It may be noted that in this procedure the operating combinations of third and first, also third and second are not required to be worked out resulting in considerable saving in computational effort. The process is repeated, till all available units are exhausted. The advantage of this approach is that having obtained the optimal way of loading k units, it is quite easy to determine the optimal manner of loading $(k + 1)$ units.

From the results obtained by the above process a unit commitment table, which shows the units in operation requiring minimum operating cost for the various loads, is prepared. The unit commitment table is prepared once and for all for a given set of units. If the load cycle on a station load changes, it will require to change the starting and stopping times of the units with the basic unit commitment table remaining unchanged.

Using the unit commitment table and increasing load in steps, the most economical station operating cost is calculated for the complete range of station capacity by equal incremental cost criterion. The result is the overall station cost characteristic in the form of a set of data points. A quadratic equation (or higher order equation, if necessary) can then be fitted to this data for later use in economic load sharing among generating stations.

Example 1.3. Consider a system having four thermal generating units with parameters listed in Table 1.1 in which operating cost characteristic is taken as

$$C_i(P_i) = \frac{1}{2} a_i P_i^2 + b_i P_i + d_i.$$

Table 1.1 : Generating unit parameters

Unit No.	*Capacity (MW)*		*Cost curve parameters (d = 0)*	
	Min.	*Max.*	*a* (Rs./MW^2)	*b* (Rs./MW)
1	1.0	12.0	0.77	23.5
2	1.0	12.0	1.60	26.5
3	1.0	12.0	2.00	30.0
4	1.0	12.0	2.50	32.0

Determine the most economical units to be committed for a load ranging from 0 MW to 9 MW with a step size of 1 MW.

Solution : Given that operating cost function

$$C_1 = \frac{1}{2} \times 0.77P_1^2 + 23.5P_1, \; C_2 = \frac{1}{2} \times 1.60P_2^2 + 26.5P_2,$$

$$C_3 = \frac{1}{2} \times 2.00P_3^2 + 30.0P_3, \; C_4 = \frac{1}{2} \times 2.50P_4^2 + 32.0P_4$$

Let the discrete form of cost function C_i is denoted by f_i. From the given data the cost function of first unit f_1 (y), $y = 0, 1, 2, 3, 4, 5, 6, 7, 8, 9$ is obtained as

$$f_1(P_1) = \frac{1}{2} \times 0.77P_1^2 + 23.5P_1, \; P_1 = 0, 1, 2, 3, 4, 5, 6, 7, 8, 9$$

therefore $f_1(0) = 0$, $f_1(1) = 23.885$, $f_1(2) = 48.54$, $f_1(3) = 73.965$, $f_1(4) = 100.16$, $f_1(5) = 127.125$, $f_1(6) = 154.86$, $f_1(7) = 183.365$, $f_1(8) = 212.64$ and $f_1(9) = 242.685$. Similarly since

$$f_2(P_2) = \frac{1}{2} \times 1.60P_2^2 + 26.5P_2,$$

therefore $f_2(0) = 0$, $f_2(1) = 27.3$, $f_2(2) = 56.2$, $f_2(3) = 86.7$, $f_2(4) = 118.8$, $f_2(5) = 152.5$, $f_2(6) = 187.8$, $f_2(7) = 224.7$, $f_2(8) = 263.5$ and $f_2(9) = 303.3$.

Now application of dynamic programming method gives optimum cost function for the two units as

$$F_2(x) = \min_{y} \{f_2(y) + F_1(x - y)\}$$

$$= \min_{y} \{f_2(y) + f_1(x - y)\}$$

Therefore

$$F_2(0) = \min\{f_2(0) + f_1(0 - 0)\} = 0 \;\; i.e., \text{ with } P_1 = 0, \; P_2 = 0$$

$$F_2(1) = \min\{[F_2(0) + f_1(1 - 0)], \; [f_2(1) + f_1(1 - 1)]\}$$

$$= \min\{[f_2(0) + f_1(1)], \; [f_2(1) + f_1(0)]\}$$

$$= \min\{(0 + 23.885), \; (27.3 + 0)\}$$

$$= \min\{23.885, \; 27.3\}$$

$$= 23.885 \text{ which is obtained with } P_1 = 1, \; P_2 = 0$$

$$F_2(2) = \min\{[f_2(0) + f_1(2 - 0)], \; [f_2(1) + f_1(2 - 1)], \; [f_2(2) + f_1(2 - 2)]\}$$

$$= \min\{[f_2(0) + f_1(2)], \; [f_2(1) + f_1(1)], \; [f_2(2) + f_1(0)]\}$$

$$= \min \{[0 + 48.54],\ [27.3 + 23.885],\ [56.2 + 0]\}$$

$$= \min \{48.54,\ 51.185,\ 56.2\}$$

$$= 48.54 \text{ which is obtained with } P_1 = 2,\ P_2 = 0.$$

Continuing similarly F_2 (3), F_2 (4),...., F_2 (9) can be obtained. Then f_3 (y), $y = 0, 1, 2, ..., 9$ can be calculated from the cost function

$$f_3 (P_3) = \frac{1}{2} \times 2.00P_3^2 + 30.0P_3,$$

and then $F_3 (x) = \min_{y} \{f_3 (y) + F_2 (x - y)\}$ for $x = 0, 1, 2, ..., 9$

knowing $F_2 (x - y)$ from previous step. Similarly F_4 (x), $x = 0, 1, 2, ..., 9$ can be computed.

The calculations can be made in tabular form more conveniently as shown in Table 1.2. Here column 2, 3, 7 and 12 are obtained from cost characteristics of the units. First the column 4, 5 and 6 are filled using dynamic programming technique. For example, for computing entry of column 6, row 2 the values of columns 2 and 3 on the two sides of the arrows indicated are added and compared, and the minimum is written in column 6. Here these values are (0 + 23.885) and (0 + 27.3) and the minimum is 23.885 which is written in column 6. As the cost 23.885 corresponds to $P_1 = 1$ and $P_2 = 0$ therefore these values are written in columns 4 and 5 respectively. Note that second arrow meeting 0 and 27.3 can be obtained by tilting top side of the first arrow (meeting 23.885 and 0) up by one and bottom side of the arrow down by one. Thus to fill the *p* load row entry in the column 6 mark an arrow with bottom in 0 load row, column 3 and top in the *p* load row, column 2, add the entries on the two sides of the arrow, tilt the top side of the arrow up by one and bottom side of the arrow down by one and add the entries on the two sides of the arrow, and continue till the top side of the arrow comes in the top row. Compare all the results obtained from additions and the least of them qualifies to be put in column 6. Corresponding values of P_1 and P_2 are written in columns 4 and 5. Once all the entries of column 6 are filled *i.e.*, when F_2 is obtained, now F_3 can be obtained by filling entries in column 11. To fill the entries of column 11, perform the same operations on columns 6, 7 and 11 as made for columns 2, 3 and 6. While filling the entries in column 11 the entries in columns 2, 3, 4 and 5 can be forgotten but to fill the entries of columns 8 and 9 help of columns 4, 5 and 6 is required. The table can be completed upto column 17 in the same manner. Columns 18, 19, 20 and

Table 1.2 : Calculations for Optimal Unit commitment using Dynamic Programming method

Load in MW	Unit-1 cost $f_1 = F_1$	Unit-2 cost f_2	Units 1 and 2 available			Unit-3 cost f_3	Units 1, 2 and 3 available				Unit-4 cost f_4	Units 1, 2, 3 and 4 available					Status of the units 1-on, 0-off			
			optimum				optimum					optimum					Unit no.			
			Load on Unit-1	Load on Unit-2	cost F_2		Load on Unit-1	Load on Unit-2	Load on Unit-3	cost F_3		Load on Unit-1	Load on Unit-2	Load on Unit-3	Load on Unit-4	cost F_4	1	2	3	4
1	2	3	4	5	6	7	8	9	10	11	12	13	14	15	16	17	18	19	20	21
0	0.000	0.000	0	0	0.000	0.000	0	0	0	0.000	0.0	0	0	0	0	0.000	0	0	0	0
1	23.885	27.300	1	0	23.885	31.000	1	0	0	23.885	33.250	1	0	0	0	23.885	1	0	0	0
2	48.540	56.200	2	0	48.540	64.000	2	0	0	48.540	69.000	2	0	0	0	48.540	1	0	0	0
3	73.965	86.700	3	0	73.965	99.000	3	0	0	73.965	107.250	3	0	0	0	73.965	1	0	0	0
4	100.160	118.800	4	0	100.160	136.000	4	0	0	100.160	148.000	4	0	0	0	100.160	1	0	0	0
5	127.125	152.500	5	0	127.125	175.000	5	0	0	127.125	191.250	5	0	0	0	127.125	1	0	0	0
6	154.860	187.800	5	1	154.425	216.000	5	1	0	154.425	237.000	5	1	0	0	154.425	1	1	0	0
7	183.365	224.700	6	1	182.160	259.000	6	1	0	182.160	285.250	6	1	0	0	182.160	1	1	0	0
8	212.640	263.200	7	1	210.665	304.000	7	1	0	210.665	336.000	7	1	0	0	210.665	1	1	0	0
9	242.685	303.300	7	2	239.565	351.000	7	2	0	239.565	389.250	7	2	0	0	239.565	1	1	0	0

21 can be filled from the columns 13, 14, 15 and 16 respectively by replacing nonzero entries by 1 and zero entries as it is.

The unit commitment table is now constructed using Table 1.2 which is given in Table 1.3.

Table 1.3 : Unit Commitment Table

Load range	***Status of the units 1-on, 0-off***			
	Unit no.			
	1	***2***	***3***	***4***
1 – 5	1	0	0	0
6 – 9	1	1	0	0

The Table 1.2 can be extended for load level upto 48 MW (maximum possible load = sum of the capacities of the units). The unit commitment table for the load varying from 0 MW to 48 MW can be obtained as given in Table 1.4.

Table 1.4 : Unit Commitment Table

Load range	***Status of the units 1-on, 0-off***			
	Unit no.			
	1	***2***	***3***	***4***
1 – 5	1	0	0	0
6 – 13	1	1	0	0
14 – 18	1	1	1	0
19 – 48	1	1	1	1

It may be noted from Table 1.2 that the optimal load distribution for 9 MW load is 7 MW on unit 1 and 2 MW on unit 2. The equal incremental cost criteria gives optimal load distribution as 7.34 MW and 1.66 MW respectively. The difference in optimal load distribution is due to the fact that the step size in optimal unit commitment has been taken as 1 MW. If higher accuracy is desired the step size may be reduced, Instead the best scheme is to restrict the use of dynamic programming method to obtain the unit commitment table for various discrete load levels, while the load sharing among committed units may then be decided by the use of the equal incremental cost criterion.

1.9 OPTIMAL GENERATION SCHEDULING (INCLUDING TRANSMISSION LOSSES)

Let C_i = cost of fuel input to ith generating station in Rs./hr

C_t = total cost of fuel input to all the stations in Rs./hr

P_i = power output of ith station in MW

P_D = total load demand of the system

P_L = total transmission loss

n = total number of stations

The total fuel cost

$$C_t = C_1 + C_2 + \ldots + C_n \quad \ldots(1.28)$$

In steady state total load demand P_D is equal to total generation minus total transmission losses therefore

$$P_D = P_1 + P_2 + \ldots + P_n - P_L \quad \ldots(1.29)$$

The Eq. (1.29) can be rewritten as

$$\sum_{i=1}^{n} P_i - P_D - P_L = 0 \quad \ldots(1.30)$$

It is required to calculate P_i, $i = 1, 2, \ldots, n$ which result in minimum total cost C_t subject to the equality constraint given by Eq. (1.30). The optimization problem can be solved by using Lagrange multiplier technique. Using this method an augmented cost function (Lagrangian) is defined as

$$\overline{C}_t = C_t - \lambda\left(\sum_{i=1}^{n} P_i - P_D - P_L\right) \quad \ldots(1.31)$$

where λ is the Lagrange multiplier.

It will be shown later in Sec. 1.10 that if the power factor of load at each bus is assumed constant then the system transmission loss P_L can be expressed as a function of active power generation at each plant. Therefore

$$P_L = f(P_1, P_2, \ldots, P_n) \quad \ldots(1.32)$$

This shows that the right hand side of the Eq. (1.31) is a function of P_i only. For optimum real power dispatch

$$\frac{\partial \bar{C}_t}{\partial P_i} = 0$$

or $$\frac{\partial C_t}{\partial P_i} - \lambda\left(1 - \frac{\partial P_L}{\partial P_i}\right) = 0$$

or $$\frac{1}{\left(1 - \dfrac{\partial P_L}{\partial P_i}\right)} \cdot \frac{\partial C_t}{\partial P_i} = \lambda \qquad \text{...(1.33)}$$

Since the cost of fuel input to ith unit C_i depends on the output of that unit P_i only therefore using Eq. (1.28)

$$\frac{\partial C_t}{\partial P_i} = \frac{dC_i}{dP_i} \quad \text{for } i = 1, 2, ..., n \qquad \text{...(1.34)}$$

From Eqs. (1.33) and (1.34)

$$\frac{1}{\left(1 - \dfrac{\partial P_L}{\partial P_i}\right)} \cdot \frac{dC_i}{dP_i} = \lambda \quad \text{for } i = 1, 2, ..., n \qquad \text{...(1.35)}$$

Since $P_L = f(P_1, P_2, ..., P_n)$ therefore if $P_i = 1, 2, ..., n$ are known, the value of P_L can be calculated. In Eqs. (1.30) and (1.35) the number of unknowns are $(n + 1)$ which are P_i, $i = 1, 2, ..., n$ and λ. The $(n + 1)$ number of equations given by Eq. (1.35) together with Eq. (1.30) can be solved simultaneously to obtain the values of the $(n + 1)$ unknowns.

The Eq. (1.35) can be written as

$$L_i \frac{dC_i}{dP_i} = \lambda, \quad i = 1, 2, ..., n \qquad \text{...(1.36)}$$

where $L_i = \dfrac{1}{\left(1 - \dfrac{\partial P_L}{\partial P_i}\right)}$ is called the penalty factor of the ith generating station.

If penalty factor L_i for each station is given, the optimal values of

$$P_i, \; i = 1, 2, ..., n$$

can be obtained by solving Eq. (1.36) together with Eq. (1.30).

The partial derivative $\frac{\partial P_L}{\partial P_i}$ appearing in Eq. (1.35) is referred to as the incremental transmission loss associated with the ith generating station. The Eq. (1.35) can be rewritten in alternative form as

$$\frac{dC_i}{dP_i} = \lambda\left(1 - \frac{\partial P_L}{\partial P_i}\right), \quad i = 1, 2, ..., n \qquad ...(1.37)$$

If incremental transmission loss $\frac{\partial P_L}{\partial P_i}$ for each station is given, the optimal values of P_i, $i = 1, 2, ..., n$ can be obtained by solving Eq. (1.37) together with Eq. (1.30).

The Eq. (1.35) and its alternative forms Eq. (1.36) and (1.37) are called exact coordination equations.

1.10 TRANSMISSION LOSS FORMULA

Consider a simple system consisting of two generating plants and one load as shown in Fig. 1.4.

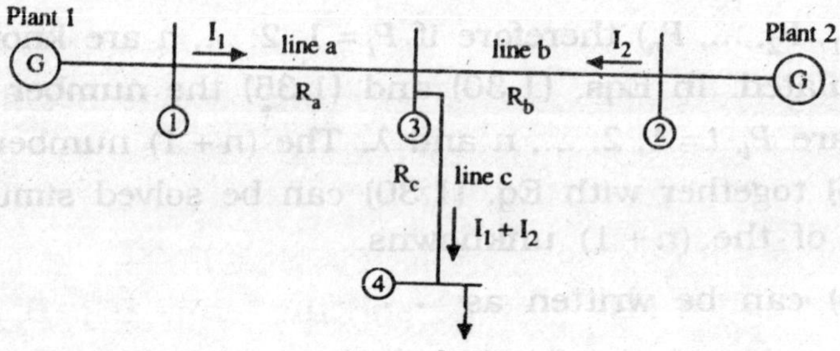

Fig. 1.4 : A simple power system

If R_a, R_b and R_c are the resistances of the lines a, b and c respectively, the total loss for the three phase transmission system is

$$P_L = 3\,|I_1|^2 R_a + 3\,|I_2|^2 R_b + 3\,|I_1 + I_2|^2 R_c \qquad ...(1.38)$$

Assume that I_1 and I_2 are in phase. Therefore

$$|I_1 + I_2| = |I_1| + |I_2| \qquad ...(1.39)$$

From Eqs. (1.38) and (1.39)

$$P_L = 3\,|I_1|^2 R_a + 3\,|I_2|^2 R_b + 3\,(|I_1|^2 + 2\,|I_1|\,|I_2| + |I_2|^2)\,R_c$$
$$= 3\,|I_1|^2 (R_a + R_c) + 3 \times 2\,|I_1|\,|I_2|\,R_c + 3\,|I_2|^2 (R_b + R_c) \qquad \text{...(1.40)}$$

If P_1 and P_2 are the three phase power outputs of plants 1 and 2 at power factors pf_1 and pf_2 and if V_1 and V_2 are the bus voltages at the plants, then

$$|I_1| = \frac{P_1}{\sqrt{3}\,|V_1|\,pf_1} \quad \text{and} \quad |I_2| = \frac{P_2}{\sqrt{3}\,|V_2|\,pf_2}$$

Substituting these in Eq. (1.40)

$$P_L = P_1^2 \frac{(R_a + R_c)}{|V_1|^2\,pf_1^2} + 2P_1\,P_2 \frac{R_c}{|V_1|\,|V_2|\,pf_1\,pf_2} + P_2^2 \frac{(R_b + R_c)}{|V_2|^2\,pf_2^2}$$
$$= P_1^2\,B_{11} + 2P_1\,P_2\,B_{12} + P_2^2\,B_{22} \qquad \text{...(1.41)}$$

where $B_{11} = \dfrac{(R_a + R_c)}{|V_1|^2\,pf_1^2}$,

$$B_{12} = \frac{R_c}{|V_1|\,|V_2|\,pf_1\,pf_2}, \text{ and}$$

$$B_{22} = \frac{(R_b + R_c)}{|V_2|^2\,pf_2^2}$$

The Eq. (1.41) is called loss formula and the terms B_{11}, B_{12} and B_{22} are called loss formula coefficients or loss coefficients or simply *B*-coefficients. The loss formula can also be written as

$$P_L = \sum_{i=1}^{2} \sum_{j=1}^{2} B_{ij}\,P_i\,P_j \qquad \text{...(1.42)}$$

where $B_{ij} = B_{ji}$.

The *B*-coefficients are constant with the variation of P_1 and P_2, only if bus voltages at the plants are maintained at constant magnitude, power factors at plants remain constant and plant output currents I_1 and I_2 are in same phase. Fortunately, the use of constant values for the loss coefficients in Eq. (1.42) gives reasonably accurate results when the coefficients are calculated for some average operating condition and if extremely wide shifts of load between plants or in total load do not occur. In practice large systems are economically loaded by calculations based on several sets of loss coefficients depending on load conditions.

Generalising for n plants the transmission loss formula can be expressed as

$$P_L = \sum_{i=1}^{n} \sum_{j=1}^{n} B_{ij} P_i P_j \quad \text{...(1.43)}$$

where $\qquad B_{ij} = B_{ji}$.

Example 1.4. For a power system having two generating stations the B-coefficients are

$$B_{11} = 0.001 \text{ MW}^{-1}, \; B_{12} = -0.0005 \text{ MW}^{-1} \text{ and } B_{22} = 0.0024 \text{ MW}^{-1}$$

and the incremental costs of the two stations are

$$\frac{dC_1}{dP_1} = 0.08P_1 + 16 \text{ Rs/MW-hr} \quad \text{...(1.44)}$$

$$\frac{dC_2}{dP_2} = 0.08P_2 + 12 \text{ Rs/MW-hr} \quad \text{...(1.45)}$$

Calculate economic outputs of the generating stations P_1 and P_2 for $\lambda = 20$. Also calculate the transmission losses and the load demand for this value of λ.

Solution : The total transmission loss is given by

$$P_L = 0.001P_1^2 + 2 \times (-0.0005) P_1 P_2 + 0.0024P_2^2 \quad \text{...(1.46)}$$

therefore
$$\frac{\partial P_L}{\partial P_1} = 0.002P_1 - 0.001P_2 \quad \text{...(1.47)}$$

$$\frac{\partial P_L}{\partial P_2} = -0.001P_1 + 0.0048P_2 \quad \text{...(1.48)}$$

For economic outputs, the outputs must satisfy the Eq. (1.35). From Eqs. (1.35), (1.47) and (1.48) and given value of λ for economic outputs

$$\frac{1}{1-(0.002P_1 - 0.001P_2)} \cdot \frac{dC_1}{dP_1} = 20 \quad \text{...(1.49)}$$

$$\frac{1}{1-(-0.001P_1+0.0048P_2)}\cdot\frac{dC_2}{dP_2}=20 \qquad ...(1.50)$$

From Eqs. (1.44) and (1.49)

$$\frac{(0.08P_1+16)}{1-(0.002P_1-0.001P_2)}=20$$

or $$0.08P_1+16=20\,(1-0.002P_1+0.001P_2)$$

or $$0.08P_1+16=20-0.04P_1+0.02P_2$$

or $$0.12P_1=4+0.02P_2$$

or $$P_1=\frac{4+0.02P_2}{0.12} \qquad ...(1.51)$$

Similarly from Eqs. (1.45) and (1.50)

$$\frac{(0.08P_2+12)}{1-(-0.001P_1+0.0048P_2)}=20$$

or $$0.08P_2+12=20\,(1+0.001P_1-0.0048P_2)$$

or $$0.176P_2=0.02P_1+8$$

Substituting value of P_1 from Eq. (1.51)

$$0.176P_2=0.02\times\frac{4+0.02P_2}{0.12}+8$$

or $$0.02112P_2=0.08+0.0004P_2+0.96$$

or $$0.02072P_2=1.04$$

or $$P_2=50.2\text{ MW}$$

substituting the value of P_2 into Eq. (1.51) gives

$$P_1=\frac{4+0.02\,(50.2)}{0.12}=41.7\text{ MW}$$

Substituting the value of P_1 and P_2 into Eq. (1.46) gives transmission loss

$$P_L=0.001\,(41.7)^2+2\,(-0.0005)\,(41.7)\,(50.2)+0.0024\,(50.2)^2$$

$$=5.7\text{ MW}$$

Therefore load demand

$$P_D = P_1 + P_2 - P_L = 50.2 + 41.7 - 5.7 = 86.2 \text{ MW}.$$

Example 1.5. A simple power system consists of two plants connected by a transmission line. The load in the system is directly connected at the bus of plant 2. When 100 MW power flows from plant 1 to plant 2 then 15 MW is lost in transmission. The incremental costs of the two plants are

$$\frac{dC_1}{dP_1} = 0.20P_1 + 22 \text{ Rs/MW-hr} \qquad \text{...(1.52)}$$

$$\frac{dC_2}{dP_2} = 0.15P_2 + 30 \text{ Rs/MW-hr} \qquad \text{...(1.53)}$$

Calculate the economic loading of plants 1 and 2 for system $\lambda = 60$. Also calculate the transmission loss and total load demand.

Solution : The given two plant system is shown in Fig. 1.5.

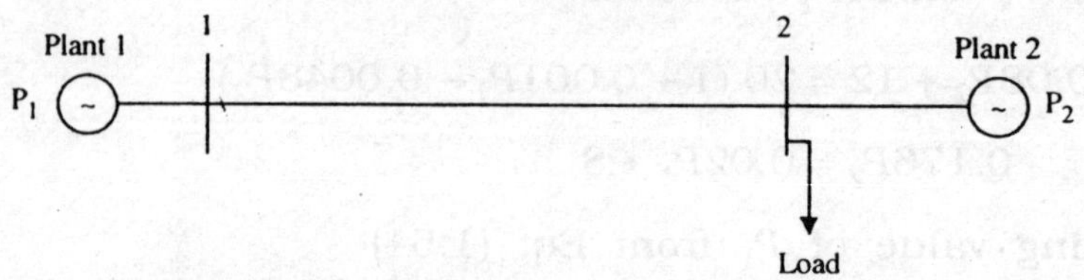

Fig. 1.5

The transmission loss for the given system is given by the loss formula

$$P_L = B_{11} P_1^2 + 2B_{12} P_1 P_2 + B_{22} P_2^2 \qquad \text{...(1.54)}$$

Since the load is at the bus of plant 2 therefore the losses depend on P_1 only and not on P_2. Therefore

$$B_{12} = 0 = B_{22}$$

substituting in Eq. (1.54)

$$P_L = B_{11} P_1^2 \qquad \text{...(1.55)}$$

Given that when $P_1 = 100$ MW, transmission loss $P_L = 15$ MW. Substituting in Eq. (1.55) gives

$$15 = B_{11}\,(100)^2$$

or $$B_{11} = 0.0015\ \text{MW}^{-1}$$

Substituting in Eq. (1.55) the transmission loss formula becomes

$$P_L = 0.0015P_1^2 \qquad \text{...(1.56)}$$

Hence, $$\frac{\partial P_L}{\partial P_1} = 0.003P_1 \qquad \text{...(1.57)}$$

and $$\frac{\partial P_L}{\partial P_2} = 0 \qquad \text{...(1.58)}$$

For economic loading of the plants, the plant outputs must satisfy the Eq. (1.35). From Eqs. (1.35), (1.57) and (1.58) and given value of λ for economic outputs

$$\frac{1}{1-(0.003)} \cdot \frac{dC_1}{dP_1} = 60 \qquad \text{...(1.59)}$$

$$\frac{1}{1-0} \cdot \frac{dC_2}{dP_2} = 60 \qquad \text{...(1.60)}$$

From Eqs. (1.52) and (1.59)

$$\frac{(0.20P_1 + 22)}{1-(0.003P_1)} = 60$$

or $$0.20P_1 + 22 = 60\,(1 - 0.003P_1)$$

or $$0.20P_1 + 22 = 60 - 0.18P_1$$

or $$0.38P_1 = 38$$

or $$P_1 = \frac{38}{0.38} = 100\ \text{MW}$$

Similarly from Eqs. (1.53) and (1.60)

$$0.15P_2 + 30 = 60$$

or $$P_2 = \frac{30}{0.15} = 200\ \text{MW}$$

Substituting value of P_1 in Eq. (1.56) the transmission loss

$$P_L = 0.0015\,(100)^2 = 15 \text{ MW}$$

and the load demand

$$P_D = P_1 + P_2 - P_L = 100 + 200 - 15 = 285 \text{ MW}.$$

REVIEW QUESTIONS

1.1 Why reserve capacity is required at generating stations?

1.2 Define various types of reserve capacities used in Power Systems.

1.3 Why interconnection of generating stations is needed?

1.4 Discuss the advantages and disadvantages of interconnection of generating stations.

1.5 What do you understand by economic loading of generating units and stations ? Explain why the fuel cost is generally taken as the operating cost in economic generation scheduling.

1.6 Define input-output curves and incremental rate curves.

1.7 Derive the necessary condition for optimal generation scheduling neglecting transmission losses.

1.8 What do you understand by the optimal unit commitment? Explain the dynamic programming method for solution of optimal unit commitment problem.

1.9 Derive the exact coordination equations for optimal generation scheduling of power plants.

1.10 Derive the transmission loss formula. Write the assumptions which are necessary for considering loss coefficients to be constant.

Chapter 2

ELEMENTS OF LOAD FREQUENCY CONTROL

In an interconnected power system, where a number of generating stations are run in parallel, it is necessary that the frequency of the system should remain constant. Constant frequency is also necessary as it affects the speed of various motors in the system which may affect quality of product in the industries.

In the power systems the load demand is never steady and changes continually with time. The load demand depends on the consumers which are independent to use the electricity in the way they like. In steady state the mechanical power input to the generators balances with the electrical load (plus losses) in the system. As soon as the system load increases the generators feed the additional load by loosing their kinetic energy and so their speed decreases reducing the system frequency. The reduction in frequency in turn reduces the speed of motors in the system and so the motor output (which is proportional to speed) drops. This reduces the system load such that the system load and input to the generators balance at some lower frequency. Reverse happens when the system load reduces. Therefore in order to keep the system frequency constant the input to the generators, steam input to thermal generators and water input to hydro-generators, must be continuously regulated to meet the load demand variations. It is required to regulate the frequency within specified narrow limits around the rated frequency, therefore control of frequency by controlling inputs to the generators is necessary. The input to the generators is generally controlled by the action of the governor which is an essential part of all types of generators.

Another objective of the system control is to keep tie line loadings fairly constant to desired value(s) according to the contracts between the various agencies/owners of the systems.

The most common load frequency control schemes are flat frequency control, flat tie-line load control, tie-line load bias control and governor control.

2.1 FLAT FREQUENCY CONTROL

In this scheme of load frequency control the job of maintaining the frequency constant is assigned to one centrally located generating station. This generating station absorbs all changes in the system load while all other generating stations carry constant loads. Within the frequency controlling generating station, one specific generating unit can be assigned the job of the automatic control of frequency. Generally, if the system is large, it is desirable to have a number of generator units co-operating in the control function.

Even if the system is large it is found that a relatively small correction in generation is required to control frequency, provided that the correction is applied before the deviation becomes appreciable. It is therefore necessary to use very sensitive frequency controller to start corrective action before the frequency departs too far from the normal. When the load swings required to regulate frequency are large in respect to the capacity of a single unit maintaining frequency, any or all the remaining units in the generating station may be placed on proportionate load control. In this case each unit has its load controller measuring its output and comparing it with that of the unit operating as frequency controller. If these loads are not distributed in the predetermined ratios, the unit load controller sends correcting impulses to its governor motor, correcting both frequency and load balance among units. The load distribution may be equal or proportionate to the unit capacity or may be divided in accordance with economic loading of units.

The main disadvantage of this type of control is that it results in random variations in tie-line loadings.

2.2 FLAT TIE-LINE LOAD CONTROL

The objective of this type of control is to keep the tie-line loading constant irrespective of load demands. In this scheme the increase in demands of an area is met by increase in generation in that area only. This type of control is used when a small system and a large system are interconnected through a tie-line. The large system maintains the system frequency and the small system is controlled to keep the tie-line loading constant. It is not suitable when two or more large systems are interconnected because with large systems the tie-line loading and frequency deviation have a tendency to swing back and forth following a load change. In this type of control, the control equipment consists of the frequency controller at the larger system and tie-line load controller-recorder at the smaller system.

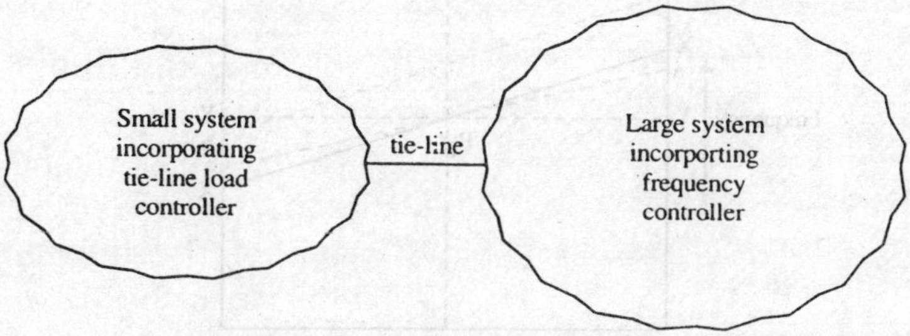

Fig. 2.1 : Flat tie-line load control

2.3 TIE-LINE LOAD BIAS CONTROL

This is the most widely used method for load frequency control of power systems having large interconnections. In this type of control, the load variations in the system are shared by all the generators in preset proportions. With this method all generating stations in the interconnected system assist in regulating frequency and tie-line power flow irrespective of where the load change has occurred.

The power system employing this method of control have control units of almost identical operating characteristics on every generating station. The control unit consists of a frequency controller and a tie-line load controller. The tie-line load controller biases the frequency controller by changing the control point until the desired relationship exists between tie-line loading and system frequency. This is explained with the help of Fig. 2.2.

In Fig. 2.2 the tie-line load bias control characteristic is represented by line *XX* and the operating point is *P*. The slope of actual characteristic is adjustable between the limits *YY* and *ZZ* such as the characteristic shown by line *aa*. The characteristic can also be moved parallel to itself such as line *bb* so that any tie-line load can be scheduled and thereafter maintained constant. If the slope of the characteristic is zero such as line *YY* the frequency of the system is maintained constant irrespective of the tie-line loading and the tie-line load varies over wide limits. If the slope of the characteristic is infinite such as line *ZZ* the tie-line load is maintained constant irrespective of the frequency. With the characteristic such as *XX*, *aa* or *bb* any tie-line load can be scheduled and thereafter maintained at the desired frequency by

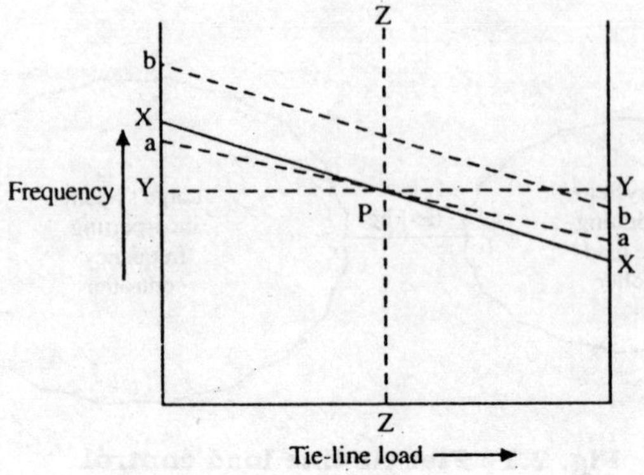

Fig. 2.2 : Tie-line load bias control

automatically adjusting generation at all the generating stations. Thus this control provides more flexibility for a wide range of operating conditions.

2.4 GOVERNOR CONTROL

The control of frequency can be done by the action of governor. The governor controls the speed of the generator turbine which is proportional to frequency. Fig. 2.3 shows basic characteristics of a governor.

Different governor settings give different operating characteristics which are parallel to each other such as lines *aa* and *bb* in Fig. 2.3. With a given

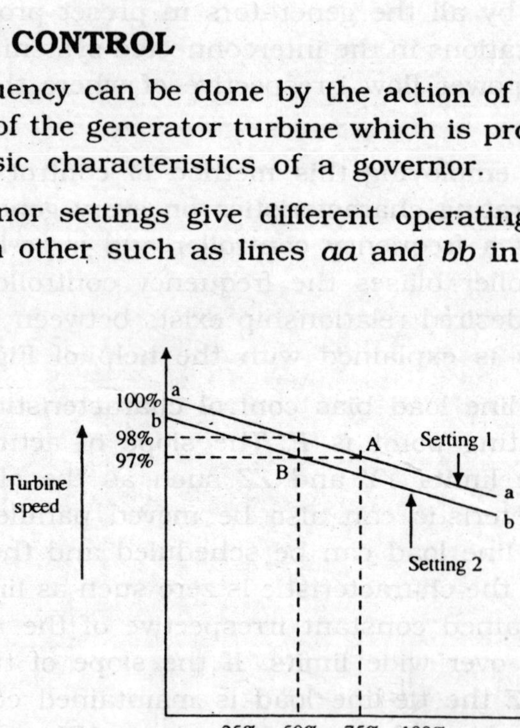

Fig. 2.3 : Characteristics of a governor

setting there is a definite relationship between turbine speed (frequency) and the load being carried by the turbine (generator load). If the load carried by the turbine increases (decreases) the speed decreases (increases). For example in Fig. 2.3 if the turbine is operating at 75% load with setting 1 the speed of the turbine is 97% of the rated and the operating point is A. If the load is reduced to 50% the speed increases to 98%. By changing now the governor setting to setting 2 the new load of 50% is taken at the original speed of 97%. Therefore the speed and hence the frequency can be maintained constant by changing governor setting appropriately. In practice this change in characteristic of the governor by changing governor setting is done by remotely operating the governor control motor from the switchboard or by automatic load controller. A turbine can thus be adjusted to carry any given load at a desired speed (frequency).

Fig. 2.4 shows schematically the speed governing system of a steam turbine.

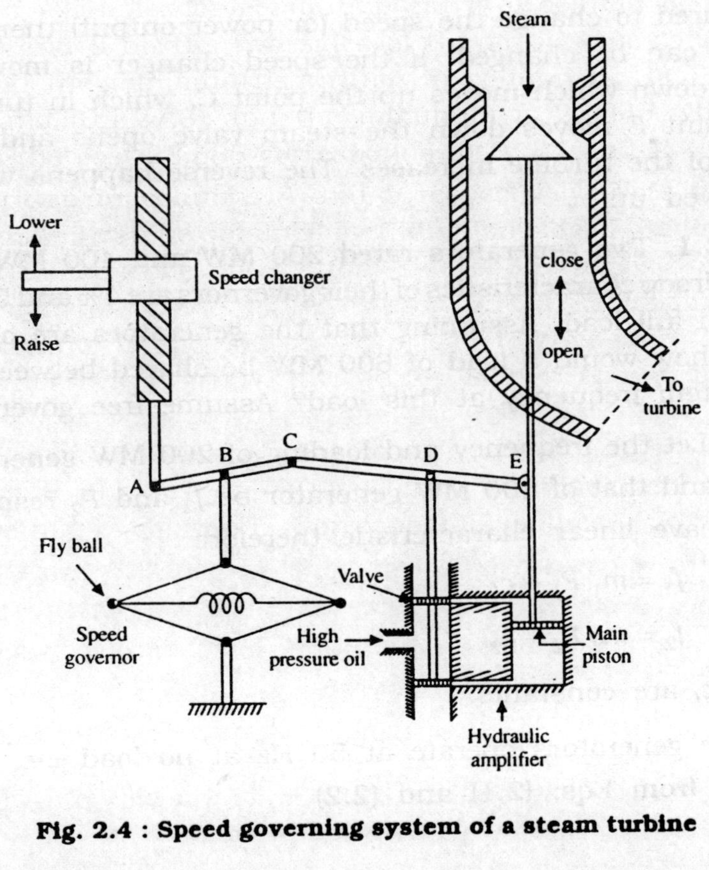

Fig. 2.4 : Speed governing system of a steam turbine

In Fig. 2.4 the speed governor consists of a flyball system in which the flyballs are connected to the turbine shaft and are rotating at the same speed as the shaft. *ABC* is a rigid link pivoted at *B* and *CDE* is another rigid link pivoted at *D*. The hydraulic amplifier amplifies the movement of point *D* at *E* *i.e.*, a small downward movement of point *D* is amplified to a large upward movement of point *E*.

The working of the speed governing system shown in Fig. 2.4 is as follows. For a given setting of governor the speed changer setting is fixed and point *A* is thus fixed. Now suppose due to a reduction in load the speed of the turbine increases. This will move the flyballs outwards due to centrifugal force and thus point *B* will be moved down by the flyball speed governor. In turn the point *C* moves down lifting point *E* up, with the movement amplified by the hydraulic amplifier. As point *E* moves up it closes steam valve reducing input to the turbine and hence the speed is reduced and brought back towards the original. The reverse happens when the speed of the turbine drops due to increase in the load on the turbine.

If it is desired to change the speed (or power output) then setting of the speed changer can be changed. If the speed changer is moved down then point *A* moves down which moves up the point *C*, which in turn moves point *E* down. As point *E* moves down the steam valve opens and the speed (or power output) of the turbine increases. The reverse happens when the speed changer is moved up.

Example 2.1. Two generators rated 200 MW and 400 MW are operating in parallel. The droop characteristics of their governors are 4% and 5%, respectively from no load to full load. Assuming that the generators are operating at 50 Hz at no load, how would a load of 600 MW be shared between them? What will be the system frequency at this load? Assume free governor operation.

Solution : Let the frequency and loading of 200 MW generator be f_1 and P_1 respectively and that of 400 MW generator be f_2 and P_2 respectively. Since the governors have linear characteristic therefore

$$f_1 = m_1 P_1 + c_1 \qquad ...(2.1)$$

$$f_2 = m_2 P_2 + c_2 \qquad ...(2.2)$$

where m_i and c_i are constants.

As both the generators operate at 50 Hz at no load *i.e.*, at $P_1 = 0$ and $P_2 = 0$ therefore from Eqs. (2.1) and (2.2)

$$50 = 0 + c_1$$

$$50 = 0 + c_2$$

giving $\qquad c_1 = 50 \qquad$ ...(2.3)

$$c_2 = 50 \qquad ...(2.4)$$

Substituting values of c_1 and c_2 from Eqs. (2.3) and (2.4) into Eqs. (2.1) and (2.2) gives

$$f_1 = m_1 P_1 + 50 \qquad ...(2.5)$$

$$f_2 = m_2 P_2 + 50 \qquad ...(2.6)$$

Given that the frequency of 200 MW generator drops by 4% when the load increases from no load to full load *i.e.*, the frequency f_1 drops to $50 - (0.04 \times 50) = 48$ Hz when load P_1 is 200 MW. Substituting these values in Eq. (2.5) gives

$$48 = m_1 \,.\, 200 + 50$$

or $\qquad 200m_1 = -2$

or $\qquad m_1 = -0.01 \qquad$ ...(2.7)

Also given that the frequency of 400 MW generator drops by 5% when the load increases from no load to full load *i.e.*, the frequency f_2 drops to $50 - (0.05 \times 50) = 47.5$ Hz when load P_2 is 400 MW. Substituting these values in Eq. (2.6) gives

$$47.5 = m_2 \,.\, 400 + 50$$

or $\qquad 400m_2 = -2.5$

or $\qquad m_2 = -0.00625 \qquad$ ...(2.8)

Substituting values of m_1 and m_2 from Eqs. (2.7) and (2.8) into Eqs. (2.5) and (2.6) gives

$$f_1 = -0.01P_1 + 50 \qquad ...(2.9)$$

$$f_2 = -0.00625P_2 + 50 \qquad ...(2.10)$$

As the two generators are operating in parallel therefore their frequency should be the same and equal to system frequency *i.e.*,

$$f_1 = f_2 = \text{system frequency} = f\,(\text{say}) \qquad ...(2.11)$$

From Eqs. (2.10) and (2.11)

$$-0.01P_1 + 50 = -0.00625P_2 + 50$$

or $$0.01P_1 = 0.00625P_2$$

or $$P_1 = 0.625P_2 \quad ...(2.12)$$

When the total load is 600 MW then

$$P_1 + P_2 = 600 \quad ...(2.13)$$

From Eqs. (2.12) and (2.13)

$$0.625P_2 + P_2 = 600$$

or $$1.625P_2 = 600$$

or $$P_2 = 369.23 \text{ MW} \quad ...(2.14)$$

Substituting the value of P_2 in Eq. (2.12) gives

$$P_1 = 0.625 \times 369.23 = 230.77 \text{ MW} \quad ...(2.15)$$

From Eqs. (2.9), (2.11) and (2.15) the system frequency

$$f = -0.01 \times 230.77 + 50 = 47.69 \text{ Hz.} \quad ...(2.16)$$

Example 2.2. Two similar 4000 kVA alternators operate in parallel. The governor of the first machine is such that frequency drops from 50 Hz on no load to 47.5 Hz on full load. The corresponding drop for the second machine is 50 Hz to 48 Hz. How will a load of 6000 kW be shared by the two machines? What will be the system frequency at this load?

Solution : Let the frequency and loading of first machine be f_1 and P_1 respectively and that of second machine be f_2 and P_2 respectively. Since the governors have linear characteristic therefore

$$f_1 = m_1 P_1 + c_1 \quad ...(2.17)$$

$$f_2 = m_2 P_2 + c_2 \quad ...(2.18)$$

where m_i and c_i are constants.

As both the generators operate at 50 Hz at no load *i.e.*, at $P_1 = 0$ and $P_2 = 0$ therefore from Eqs. (2.17) and (2.18)

$$50 = 0 + c_1$$

$$50 = 0 + c_2$$

giving $$c_1 = 50 \qquad ...(2.19)$$

$$c_2 = 50 \qquad ...(2.20)$$

Substituting values of c_1 and c_2 from Eqs. (2.19) and (2.20) into Eqs. (2.17) and (2.18) gives

$$f_1 = m_1 P_1 + 50 \qquad ...(2.21)$$

$$f_2 = m_2 P_2 + 50 \qquad ...(2.22)$$

Given that the frequency of first machine f_1 drops to 47.5 Hz when load P_1 is 4000 kVA. Substituting these values in Eq. (2.21) gives

$$47.5 = m_1 . 4000 + 50$$

or $$4000m_1 = -2.5$$

or $$m_1 = -0.000625 \qquad ...(2.23)$$

Also given that the frequency of second machine f_2 drops to 48 Hz when load P_2 is 4000 kVA. Substituting these values in Eq. (2.22) gives

$$48 = m_2 . 4000 + 50$$

or $$4000m_2 = -2$$

or $$m_2 = -0.0005 \qquad ...(2.24)$$

Substituting values of m_1 and m_2 from Eqs. (2.23) and (2.24) into Eqs. (2.21) and (2.22) gives

$$f_1 = -0.000625P_1 + 50 \qquad ...(2.25)$$

$$f_2 = -0.0005P_2 + 50 \qquad ...(2.26)$$

As the two generators are operating in parallel therefore their frequency should be the same and equal to system frequency *i.e.*,

$$f_1 = f_2 = \text{system frequency} = f \text{ (say)} \qquad ...(2.27)$$

From Eqs. (2.26) and (2.27)

$$-0.000625P_1 + 50 = -0.0005P_2 + 50$$

or $$0.000625P_1 = 0.0005P_2$$

or $$P_1 = 0.8P_2 \qquad ...(2.28)$$

When the total load is 6000 kW then

$$P_1 + P_2 = 6000 \quad \text{...(2.29)}$$

From Eqs. (2.28) and (2.29)

$$0.8P_2 + P_2 = 6000$$

or
$$1.8P_2 = 6000$$

or
$$P_2 = 3333.33 \text{ kW} \quad \text{...(2.30)}$$

Substituting the value of P_2 in Eq. (2.28) gives

$$P_1 = 0.8 \times 3333.33 = 2666.67 \text{ kW} \quad \text{...(2.31)}$$

From Eqs. (2.25), (2.27) and (2.31) the system frequency

$$f = -\,0.000625 \times 2666.67 + 50 = 48.33 \text{ Hz.} \quad \text{...(2.32)}$$

REVIEW QUESTIONS

2.1 What is the need of load frequency control in power systems? How the load frequency control is achieved? What are the objectives of load frequency control?

2.2 Discuss the Flat Frequency Control method for load frequency control in power systems. Why is it necessary to use very sensitive frequency controller in this type of control?

2.3 Explain Flat Tie Line Load Control method of load frequency control in power systems with its merits and demerits.

2.4 Discuss the Tie-Line Load Bias Control method of load frequency control in power systems.

2.5 Discuss the Governor Control.

Chapter 3

VOLTAGE CONTROL

Practically all equipments used in power systems are rated for a certain voltage with a permissible limit of voltage variations. Therefore voltage at various buses in the power system must be controlled within a specified regulation limit. At heavy loads the voltage drop in transmission lines and transformers may be too large which may cause voltage magnitude at receiving end to violate its lower permissible limit. At light loads the voltage magnitude at receiving end may be higher than the sending end due to Ferranti Effect and it may violate the upper permissible limit. The control of voltage at receiving end requires either reduction of the voltage drop/rise or compensation of it to bring its value within the permissible limits.

In addition to the voltage magnitude, sometimes, the voltage angle also becomes important in interconnected power systems. In systems where several parallel paths are existing for power flow to a point, the active power flow through a transmission line meeting this point largely depends on the difference in the angle of voltages at the two ends. This difference and hence the power flow through the line can be controlled by phase angle control of the voltage.

In this chapter various methods of voltage magnitude control and voltage angle control are discussed.

3.1 METHODS OF VOLTAGE CONTROL

The voltages at the various buses in a power system depend upon the voltage drop in the transmission lines and transformers. It is possible to control the voltage at the various buses by either compensating the voltage drop or reducing the voltage drop.

One of the methods to compensate the voltage drop in transmission lines and transformers is the use of tap changing transformers in power systems, instead of fixed ratio transformers. The taps may be adjusted to control the voltage at various buses in the system.

To quantify the voltage drop in transmission lines and transformers consider a simple two bus system connected by a transmission line and/or transformer with total reactance X between the two buses as shown in Fig. 3.1 in which a generator is connected at sending end and a load is connected at receiving end.

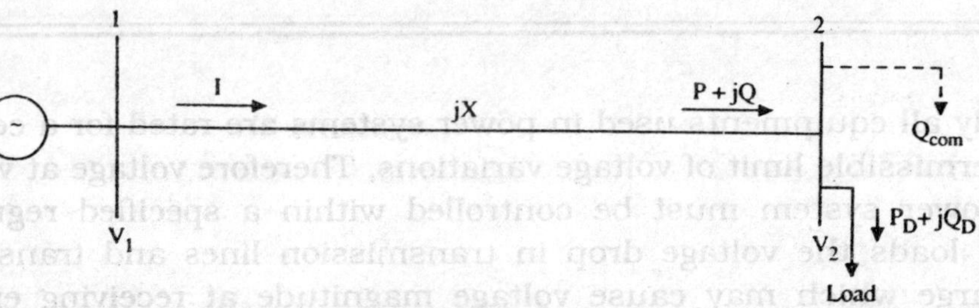

Fig. 3.1 : A simple two bus system

Let the voltage at sending end bus be V_1 and the voltage at receiving end bus be V_2. Also let the transmission line and/or transformer connecting the two buses is having negligible resistance as compared to its reactance which is usually the case. Let power $P + jQ$ is received at the receiving end and the current flowing through the line be I. Therefore

$$P + jQ = V_2 I^*$$

or $$I = \left[\frac{P+jQ}{V_2}\right]^* = \frac{P-jQ}{V_2^*} \qquad \text{...(3.1)}$$

where $[\,]^*$ is complex conjugate of [ ].

Also $$V_2 = V_1 - I\,(jX) \qquad \text{...(3.2)}$$

From Eqs. (3.1) and (3.2)

$$V_2 = V_1 - \left[\frac{P-jQ}{V_2^*}\right] jX$$

or $$V_1 = V_2 + \left[\frac{QX + jPX}{V_2^*}\right] \qquad \text{...(3.3)}$$

Taking receiving end bus as reference bus then $V_2 = |V_2| \angle 0$ and therefore

$$V_2^* = V_2 \qquad \ldots(3.4)$$

From Eqs. (3.3) and (3.4)

$$V_1 = V_2 + \left[\frac{QX + jPX}{V_2}\right]$$

or
$$V_1 = \left[V_2 + \frac{Qx}{V_2}\right] + j\frac{PX}{V_2}$$

or
$$|V_1| \angle \delta = \left[|V_2| + \frac{QX}{|V_2|}\right] + j\frac{PX}{|V_2|} \qquad \ldots(3.5)$$

where
$$V_1 = |V_1| \angle \delta.$$

In a practical power system the difference in phase angle of voltages across individual transmission lines and/or transformers is usually very small. Therefore practically

$$\frac{PX}{|V_2|} << \left[|V_2| + \frac{QX}{|V_2|}\right] \text{ and } \delta \approx 0$$

Substituting in Eq. (3.5) gives

$$|V_1| = \left[|V_2| + \frac{QX}{|V_2|}\right]$$

Therefore the voltage drop

$$|V_1| - |V_2| = \frac{QX}{|V_2|} \qquad \ldots(3.6)$$

From Eq. (3.6) it may be concluded that in order to keep the magnitude of receiving end voltage $|V_2|$ fixed for a fixed voltage magnitude at sending end $|V_1|$, the voltage drop ($QX/|V_2|$) must remain constant. The only variable in voltage drop ($QX/|V_2|$) is the reactive power flow at receiving end, Q, which varies due to variation of reactive power demand at receiving end, Q_D. If the variation in Q_D can be compensated by some means such that Q remains fixed then the voltage V_2 can be held constant. The reactive power compensation Q_{com} needed is given by the expression

$$Q = Q_D + Q_{com}$$

or $$Q_{com} = Q - Q_D \qquad \ldots(3.7)$$

If Q_D is small, such as during underloads, the Q_{com} is positive *i.e.*, a sink of reactive power, a shunt inductor is required for compensation. If Q_D is large, such as during heavy loads, the Q_{com} is negative *i.e.*, a source of reactive power, a shunt capacitor is required for compensation.

The shunt inductors employed for reactive power compensation are also called commonly as shunt reactors. The shunt reactors may be considered as source of lagging VAR and shunt capacitor as source of leading VAR.

Instead of shunt inductors and capacitors, synchronous condensers may also be used for generation or absorption of reactive power at receiving end to control the voltage. The synchronous condensers are unloaded synchronous motors whose excitation is controlled to generate or absorb the required amount of reactive power.

From Eq. (3.6) it may also be concluded that in order to keep the receiving end voltage constant for fixed $|V_1|$, another possibility is that the product $Q \cdot X$ may be kept constant. This is achieved by introducing series capacitors which reduce the net reactance of the system. Since the voltage drop is more for larger reactive power demand (larger reactive power flow) the voltage drop and hence voltage at receiving end $|V_2|$ can be controlled by switching in suitable series capacitors.

Summarising, following methods are used for voltage control :

1. Tap changing transformers
2. Shunt capacitors and shunt reactors
3. Synchronous condensers
4. Series capacitors.

3.2 TAP CHANGING TRANSFORMERS

One of the methods of voltage control is through the use of tap changing transformers. Almost all transformers in power system are provided with taps on primary or secondary winding for adjusting the ratio of transformation for voltage control. Taps are usually provided on the high voltage winding to enable a fine control of voltage and reduce arcing problem. Generally the tap changing can be done only when the transformer is in de-energised state. In the transformers having on-load tap changer, the tap changing is also possible when the transformer is in energised state. Such transformers are known as tap changing under load (TCUL) transformers. These transformers make it possible to maintain a constant voltage level on important buses in the system.

A transformer does not generate or absorb reactive power for voltage control. By changing the tap positions the reactive power flows through the transformer and associated lines change such that on one side of the transformer the voltage increases but at the same time on the other side the voltage reduces.

Fig. 3.2 shows a transmission line having tap changing transformers at its two ends.

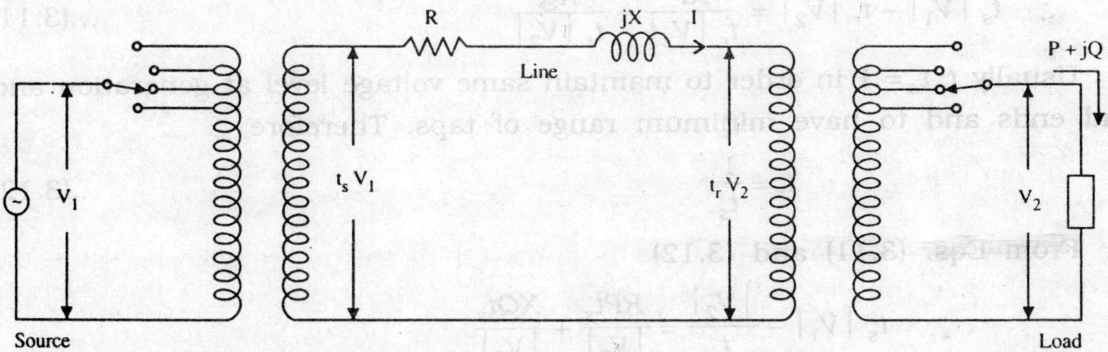

Fig. 3.2 : A transmission line with tap changing transformers at the two ends

Let the impedance of the transformers can be lumped alongwith the line impedance and the total impedance be $R + jX$ as shown in Fig. 3.2. Let t_s and t_r be the fraction of the nominal transformation *i.e.*, tap ratio/nominal ratio e.g. a transformer at receiving end with nominal ratio 132/33 kV when tapped to transform 132/36 kV has $t_r = (36/33) = 1.09$. Let V_1 and V_2 be the nominal voltages at the sending end and receiving end respectively. When taps are used, the actual sending end and receiving end voltages would be $t_s V_1$ and $t_r V_2$ respectively as shown in Fig. 3.2. Let the load at receiving end be $P + jQ$ which requires I current to flow through the transmission and the transformer as shown in Fig. 3.2. The voltage drop in transformer and transmission line can be determined from the same formula as used for transformer and can be written as

$$t_s |V_1| - t_r |V_2| = |I| \, R \cos \phi + |I| \, X \sin \phi \qquad \ldots(3.8)$$

where ϕ is the power factor angle of load and is given by

$$\phi = \tan^{-1}\frac{Q}{P}, \text{ if load is } P + jQ.$$

Therefore $$|I| \cos\phi = \frac{P}{t_r |V_2|} \quad ...(3.9)$$

and $$|I| \sin\phi = \frac{Q}{t_r |V_2|} \quad ...(3.10)$$

From Eqs. (3.8), (3.9) and (3.10)

$$t_s |V_1| - t_r |V_2| = \frac{P}{t_r |V_2|} R + \frac{Q}{t_r |V_2|} X$$

or $$t_s |V_1| - t_r |V_2| = \frac{RP}{t_r |V_2|} + \frac{XQ}{t_r |V_2|} \quad ...(3.11)$$

Usually $t_r t_s = 1$ in order to maintain same voltage level at generation and load ends and to have minimum range of taps. Therefore

$$t_r = \frac{1}{t_s} \quad ...(3.12)$$

From Eqs. (3.11) and (3.12)

$$t_s |V_1| - \frac{|V_2|}{t_s} = \frac{RPt_s}{|V_2|} + \frac{XQt_s}{|V_2|}$$

or $$t_s \left[|V_1| - \frac{RP}{|V_2|} - \frac{XQ}{|V_2|} \right] = \frac{|V_2|}{t_s}$$

or $$t_s |V_1| \left[1 - \frac{(RP + XQ)}{|V_1| \ |V_2|} \right] = \frac{|V_2|}{t_s}$$

or $$t_s^2 \left[1 - \frac{(RP + XQ)}{|V_1| \ |V_2|} \right] = \frac{|V_2|}{|V_1|}$$

or $$t_s = \sqrt{\frac{|V_2|}{|V_1|} \left[\frac{1}{1 - \dfrac{RP + XQ}{|V_1| \ |V_2|}} \right]} \quad ...(3.13)$$

For complete compensation $|V_1| = |V_2|$ and therefore

$$t_s = \sqrt{\frac{1}{1 - \dfrac{RP + XQ}{|V_1|^2}}} \quad ...(3.14)$$

The value of t_s can be calculated using Eq. (3.14) and then the value of t_r can be calculated using Eq. (3.12).

In a large interconnected system it is not possible to determine the tap setting by the simple method described above. The tap setting in large interconnected system is determined by a load flow study in which a provision for variable taps is made and final tap setting is obtained with the solution.

Example 3.1. A 220 kV line has tap changing transformers at both ends. The transformer at the sending end has a nominal ratio 11/220 kV and that at the receiving end 220/11 kV. The line impedance is $20 + j60$ ohms and the load at the receiving end is 100 MVA, 0.8 power factor lagging. If the product of the two off-nominal tap settings is 1, find the tap settings to give 11 kV at load bus.

Solution : The calculations can be done either in single phase or three phase. It may be noted from Eq. (3.14) that the expression is true for three phase as well as single phase. The calculations will be performed here in three phase.

Given :

Transmission line voltage $|V_1| = |V_2| = 220$ kv (line-to-line)

$$= 220 \times 10^3 \text{ volts}$$

Resistance of line $R = 20$ ohms

Reactance of line $X = 60$ ohms

Load power $(\sqrt{3}\ V.\ I) = 100$ MVA $= 100 \times 10^6$ VA

Load power factor $\cos\phi = 0.8$ lagging

Therefore

Real power demand $P = \sqrt{3}\,VI\cos\phi = 100 \times 10^6 \times 0.8 = 80 \times 10^6$ Watt

Reactive power demand $Q = \sqrt{3}\,VI\sin\phi = 100 \times 10^6 \times \sin(\cos^{-1} 0.8)$

$$= 60 \times 10^6 \text{ VAR}$$

From Eq. (3.14) tap setting at sending end

$$t_s = \sqrt{\frac{1}{1 - \dfrac{(20 \times 80 \times 10^6 + 60 \times 60 \times 10^6)}{(220 \times 10^3)^2}}}$$

$$= 1.058$$

and using Eq. (3.12) the tap setting at receiving end

$$t_r = \frac{1}{t_s} = \frac{1}{1.058} = 0.945.$$

3.3 ON-LOAD TAP CHANGER

The basic principle of on-load tap changer is explained with the help of the schematic circuit diagram shown in Fig. 3.3.

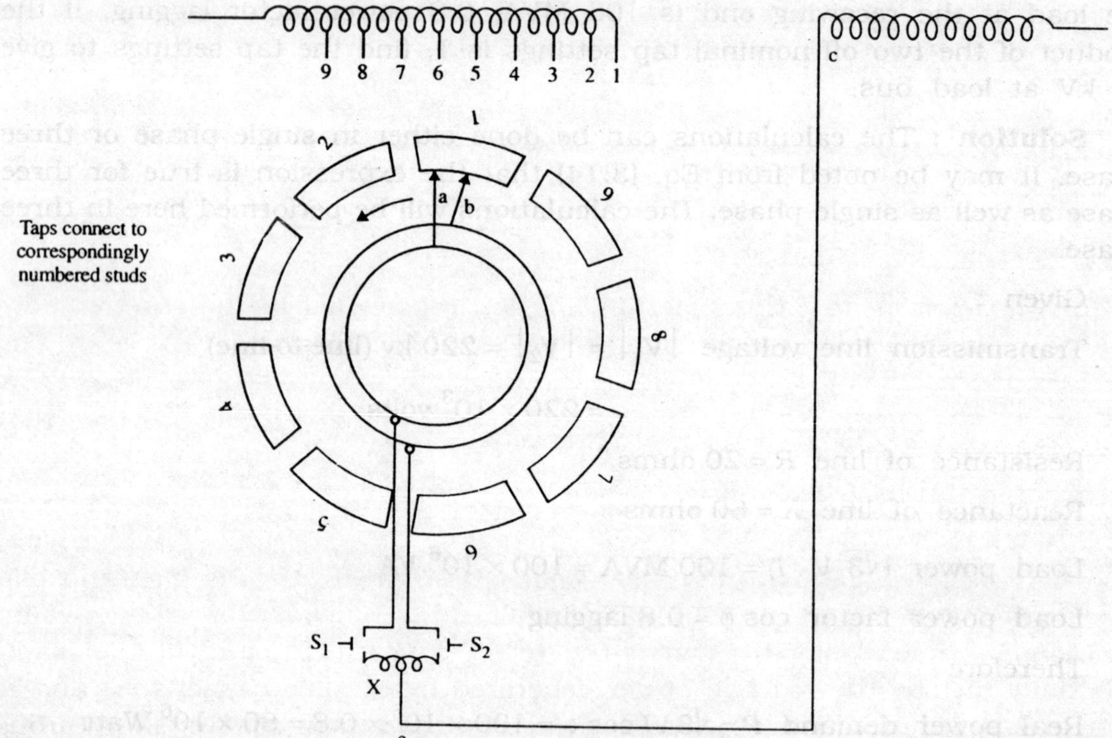

Fig. 3.3 : On-load tap changer

The essential feature of the on-load tap changer is the small reactor X which is inserted to prevent short-circuiting a section of the main winding when the movable fingers a and b are in contact with adjacent segments of the dial switch. In the position of the dial switch shown in Fig. 3.3, all turns of the main winding are in service. The load current from tap 1 reaches point *c* through reactor *X*; half of the load current enters in the reactor *X* through switch S_1 and the other half through switch S_2. The voltage drop in the reactor *X* is insignificant because of its very small leakage reactance.

Assume now that the voltage required is less than that represented by tap 1. The contact fingers *a* and *b* shown in Fig. 3.3 are rotated anti-clockwise by the tap-changing mechanism, but before finger *a* leaves stud 1, the switch S_1 opens, thereby preventing arcing at the dial. When finger *a* establishes contact with stud 2, the switch S_1 again closes, and the reactor *X* is bridged across taps 1 and 2. The potential at point *c* of the reactor is then midway between the potentials of taps 1 and 2.

If further reduction of voltage is required, the anti-clockwise rotation of fingers *a* and *b* is continued, but just before finger *b* leaves stud 1, switch S_2 is opened. The switch S_2 is again closed when finger *b* establishes contact with stud 2. The reactor *X* is then again short circuited and the potential of point *c* becomes the same as that of tap 2.

3.4 SHUNT CAPACITORS AND REACTORS

The voltage drop in a transmission line is proportional to the reactive power flowing through the line. If the reactive power flow is positive *i.e.*, it flows from sending end to the receiving end, then the voltage drop is positive and receiving end voltage is less than sending end voltage. If the reactive power flow is negative *i.e.*, it flows from receiving end to sending end, then the voltage drop is negative and receiving end voltage is higher than the sending end voltage.

For high voltage transmission lines the line capacitance is high and plays a significant role in voltage conditions of the receiving end. When a high voltage transmission line is loaded then the reactive power demand of the load is partially met by the reactive power generated by the line capacitance and the remaining reactive power demand is met by the reactive power flow through the line from sending end to the receiving end.

When the load is high then a large reactive power flows from sending end to the receiving end resulting in a large voltage drop in the line. To improve the voltage at the receiving end shunt capacitors may be connected at the receiving end to generate and feed the reactive power to the load so that reactive power flow through the line and consequently the voltage drop in the line reduces. To control the receiving end voltage a bank of capacitors (large number of capacitors connected in parallel) is installed at the receiving end and a number of capacitors are switched in during high load conditions depending upon the load demand. Thus the capacitors provide leading vars to partially meet reactive power demand of the load to control the voltage. If $X_C = (1/\omega C)$ be the reactance of the shunt capacitor then the reactive power generated or leading VAR supplied by the capacitor

$$Q_C = \frac{|V_2|^2}{X_C} = |V_2|^2 \omega C \qquad ...(3.15)$$

where $|V_2|$ is the magnitude of receiving end voltage.

When the load is small then the load reactive power demand may even be lesser than the reactive power generated by the line capacitance. Under these conditions the reactive power flow through the line becomes negative *i.e.*, the reactive power flows from receiving end to the sending end, and the receiving end voltage is higher than the sending end voltage. To control the voltage at the receiving end it is necessary to absorb or sink reactive power at the receiving end. This is achieved by connecting shunt inductors, commonly called shunt reactors, at the receiving end. The shunt reactor provide necessary lagging vars to control the voltage. If the reactance of the shunt reactor be $X_L = \omega L$ then the reactive power absorbed or lagging VAR supplied by the shunt reactor

$$Q_L = \frac{|V_2|^2}{X_L} = \frac{|V_2|^2}{\omega L} \qquad ...(3.16)$$

where $|V_2|$ is the magnitude of receiving end voltage.

To control the receiving end voltage generally one shunt inductor (reactor) is installed at the receiving end and switched in during the light load conditions. Usually the reactance and hence reactive power capacity of the inductor is fixed. To meet the variable reactive power demands requisite number of shunt capacitors are switched in, in addition to the shunt inductor, which results in adjustable reactive power absorption by the combination.

In construction the shunt reactors (inductors) are identical to a power transformer, except for their cores. They have similar windings, tanks, bushings, radiators etc. An air gap is provided within the reactor core to prevent magnetic saturation. However, this increases core vibration and noise.

The shunt capacitors and reactors are usually rated at 11 kV and are commonly connected to the tertiary winding of power transformers at the sub-stations.

Example 3.2. At a 33 KV substation of 3-phase 50 Hz power system 3 MVAR reactive power generation is required during heavy loadings to increase the voltage to the desired level. Calculate capacitance to be connected in each phase to satisfy the requirement.

Solution : Given : Reactive power of the shunt capacitors

$$Q_C = 3 \text{ MVAR} = 3 \times 10^6 \text{ VAR}$$

Frequency of the system

$$f = 50 \text{ Hz}$$

Voltage at the bus

$$|V_2| = 33 \text{ kV} = 33 \times 10^3 \text{ Volts (line-to-line)}$$

From Eq. (3.15), $Q_C = |V_2|^2 \omega C = |V_2|^2 \times 2\pi f \times C$

where C is the capacitance per phase of the shunt capacitor.

Substituting the given values

$$3 \times 10^6 = (33 \times 10^3)^2 \times 2\pi \times 50 \times C$$

or $$C = \frac{3 \times 10^6}{(33 \times 10^3)^2 \times 2\pi \times 50} = 8.769 \times 10^{-6} \text{ Ferad} = 8.769 \mu F.$$

Example 3.3. At a 400 KV substation of 3-phase 50 Hz power system 80 MVAR reactors are to be installed. Calculate inductance of the reactors to be connected in each phase.

Solution : Given : Reactive power of the shunt reactors

$$Q_L = 80 \text{ MVAR} = 80 \times 10^6 \text{ VAR}$$

Frequency of the system

$$f = 50 \text{ Hz}$$

Voltage at the bus

$$|V_2| = 400 \text{ kV} = 400 \times 10^3 \text{ Volts (line-to-line)}$$

From Eq. (3.16)

$$Q_L = \frac{|V_2|^2}{\omega L} = \frac{|V_2|^2}{2\pi f L}$$

where L is the inductance per phase of the shunt reactor.

Substituting the given values

$$80 \times 10^6 = \frac{(400 \times 10^3)^2}{2\pi \times 50 \times L}$$

or
$$L = \frac{(400 \times 10^3)^2}{2\pi \times 50 \times 80 \times 10^6} = 6.366 \text{ Henery.}$$

3.5 SERIES CAPACITORS

Long transmission lines have a very high series inductive reactance. This reactance causes a large voltage drop in the line and consequently voltage at receiving end is poor. To reduce the voltage drop in the line a series capacitor is connected at suitable location along the line. By connecting the series capacitor the net series reactance and consequently voltage drop between sending end and receiving end reduces so the voltage at receiving end improves. If the series inductive reactance of the line is $X_L = \omega L$ and reactance of the series capacitor is $X_C = (1/\omega C)$ then the net series reactance between the sending end and receiving end becomes $X = X_L - X_C$. The voltage drop without series capacitor is IX_L and with series capacitor it is $I(X_L - X_C) = IX_L - IX_C$. Thus the voltage drop IX_L in line reactance is compensated by the voltage rise in the series capacitor by the amount IX_C. The factor $\frac{IX_C}{IX_L} = \frac{X_C}{X_L}$ is known as degree of compensation. Studies on transmission systems have shown that in view of line cost, the limitation of lines operating in parallel and problems of system protection, the economic degree of compensation lies in the range of 40% to 70%.

The series capacitor(s) can be located at mid-point of the line or at (1/3) distance from sending end and receiving end or at one or both ends of the line. The capacitor stations are generally unattended type.

The shunt capacitor and series capacitor both generate reactive power to control the voltage. The reactive power generated by the shunt capacitor is proportional to square of receiving end voltage whereas the reactive power generated by series capacitor is proportional to square of the load current. Therefore the reactive power generated by the shunt capacitor is independent of load whereas the reactive power generated by the series capacitor depends upon the load. Hence the amount of reactive power generated by series capacitor automatically adjusts with the load. This is an advantage of series capacitor over shunt capacitor.

3.6 THYRISTORISED STATIC VAR COMPENSATORS

The load on EHV lines varies in wide limits requiring both inductive and capacitive shunt compensation and the type and amount of compensation depends on the load. Though the variable shunt compensation, both capacitive and inductive, can be achieved efficiently with the help of synchronous condensers, but due to the inherent disadvantages of rotating devices these are not preferred. The static inductors and capacitors can provide the inductive and capacitive compensation but the compensation is not variable continuously and is in steps. The thyristorised static VAR compensators employ static inductors and capacitors controlled by thyristors to provide continuously variable shunt compensation. The various configurations of thyristorised static VAR compensators are described below.

3.6.1 Thyristor Controlled Reactor (TCR)-Fixed Capacitor (FC) Compensator

The TCR-FC compensator is shown in Fig. 3.4. In this compensator a thyristor controlled reactor and two or more fixed capacitors are used to provide both

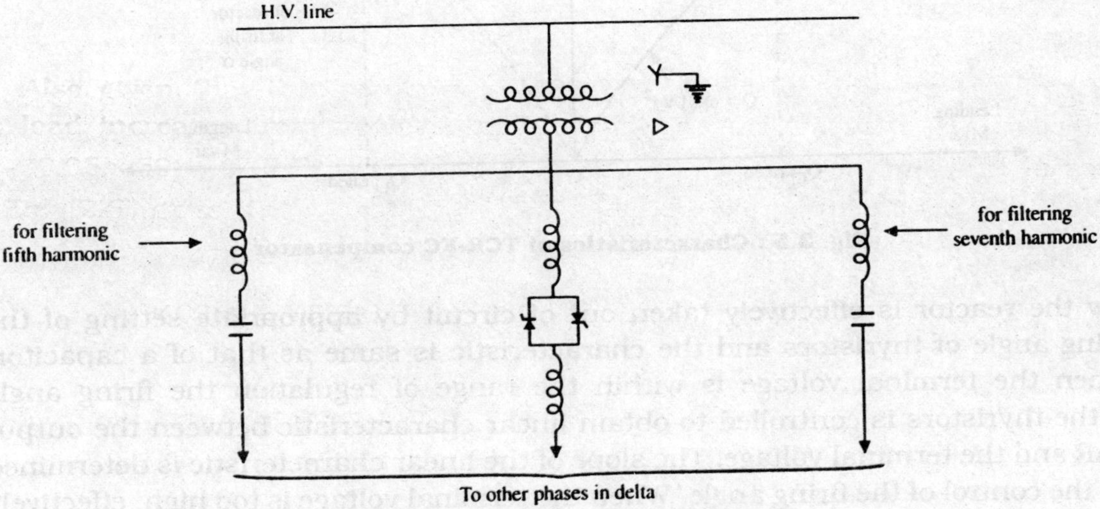

Fig. 3.4 : The TCR-FC compensator

inductive and capacitive compensation. The compensator provides continuously controllable lagging to leading vars through thyristor control of reactor current. The reactor is generally rated larger than the total of fixed capacitance therefore net lagging vars can also be supplied. The variation of current through the reactor is obtained by phase angle control of back to back pairs of thyristors connected in series with the reactor. The phase angle control produces harmonics. Since there are 6 thyristors for the three phases, 6-pulse operation is achieved which produce substantial fifth and seventh harmonics in addition to third harmonics. The thyristor controlled reactor, fixed capacitor and coupling transformer secondary are arranged in delta to cancel third harmonics. The small reactors usually included in the fixed capacitor branches tune these branches as filters for the fifth and seventh harmonics.

The reactive power output versus terminal voltage steady state characteristic of the compensator is shown in Fig. 3.5. When the terminal voltage is too

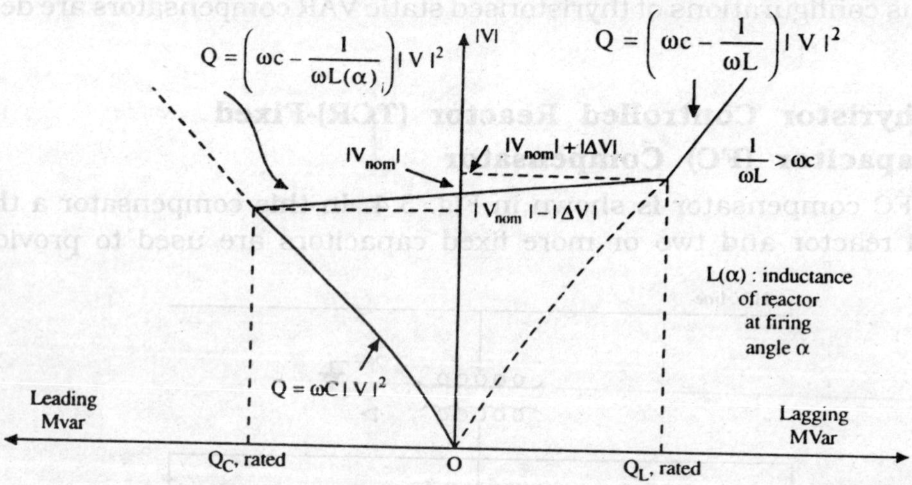

Fig. 3.5 : Characteristics of TCR-FC compensator

low the reactor is effectively taken out of circuit by appropriate setting of the firing angle of thyristors and the characteristic is same as that of a capacitor. When the terminal voltage is within the range of regulation the firing angle of the thyristors is controlled to obtain linear characteristic between the output VAR and the terminal voltage. The slope of the linear characteristic is determined by the control of the firing angle. When the terminal voltage is too high, effectively whole of the reactor capacity is in service and the characteristic is same as that of an inductor.

3.6.2 Thyristor Controlled Transformer (TCT) compensator

The TCT compensator is shown in Fig. 3.6. The compensator is similar to TCR-FC compensator in principle. The TCT compensator consists of a trans-

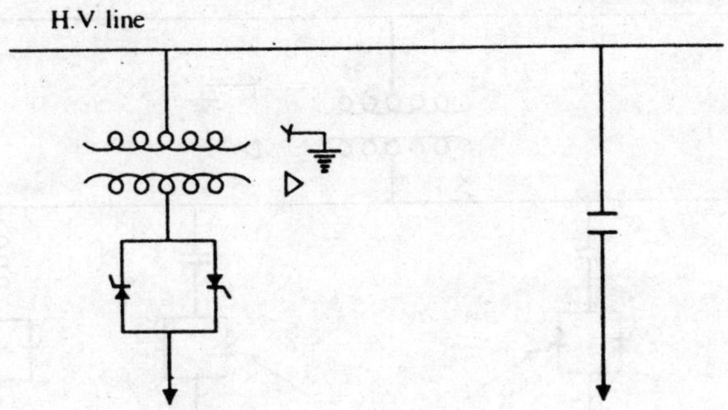

Fig. 3.6 : The TCT compensator

former of special design with almost 100% leakage reactance which is controlled on the secondary side by thyristors. Third harmonics are eliminated by connecting the three phases of secondary in delta. This compensator has better overload capacity and can with-stand severe transient overvoltages. However it is more costly as compared to the TCR-FC compensator.

3.6.3 Thyristor Switched Capacitor (TSC)-Thyristor Controlled Reactor (TCR) compensator

The TSC-TCR compensator is shown in Fig. 3.7.

The compensator consists of a thyristor controlled reactor(s) and *n* thyristor switched capacitors. The number *n* of the capacitors is determined from practical considerations which include maximum compensation required, current rating of thyristor switches and operating voltage level etc. The anti-parallel thyristors in series with the reactor(s) are capable of continuously controlling the current in the reactor from zero to maximum value. The anti-parallel thyristor switches in series with capacitors allow the switching in of the required number of capacitors in discrete steps. A small number of fixed capacitors alongwith a series reactor with each capacitor are used as tuned filters for harmonics.

The TSC-TCR compensator has the capability to provide both leading and lagging VARs rapidly and independently. The reactive power output versus terminal voltage characteristic of the compensator is similar to the characteristic of TCR-FC compensator. The advantages of TSC-TCR compensator over TCR-FC are the improved performance during large system disturbances and lower losses.

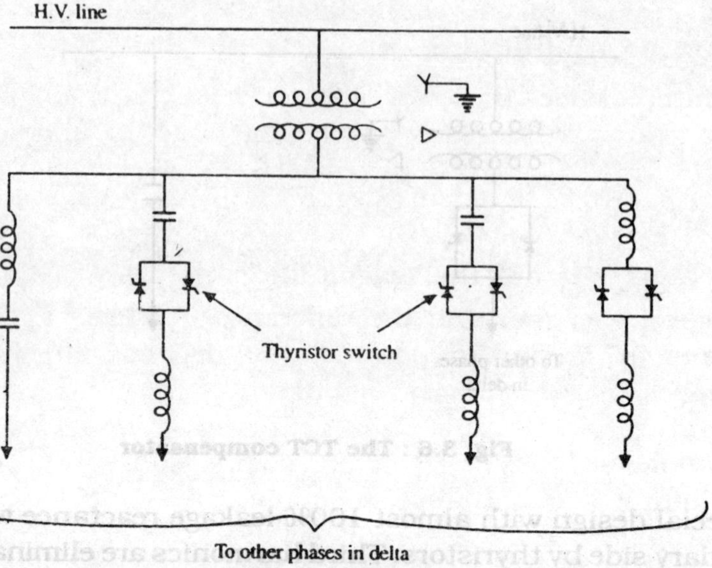

Fig. 3.7 : The TSC-TCR compensator

However, the TSC-TCR compensator is about 15-20% more costly as compared to the TCR-FC compensator.

3.6.4 Mechanically Switched Capacitor (MSC)-Thyristor Controlled Reactor (TCR) compensator

The MSC-TCR compensator is similar to TSC-TCR compensator except that it uses conventional mechanical or SF_6 switches instead of thyristors to switch the capacitors. The MSC-TCR compensator is more economical when there are a large number of capacitors to be switched, as compared to TSC-TCR compensator. The time of switching is however longer in MSC-TCR compensator as compared to TSC-TCR compensator which may adversely effect the transient stability of the power system.

3.7 PHASE ANGLE CONTROL

The need for phase-angle control arises when two transmission lines, having different impedances, but supplied from a single source, are required to be connected together at a distant bus. In these situations, the line voltages at the receiving ends of the two lines may be out of phase. If the receiving ends of the lines are connected together directly to the same bus then a circulating current may flow in the two parallel lines. By inserting a phase-angle control unit at receiving end of one of the lines, the division of current between the two lines can be controlled.

In an interconnected power system network the flow of active power P through a transmission line connecting buses p and q is given by

$$P = \frac{|V_p|\;|V_q|}{X}\sin\delta$$

where $|V_p|$ and $|V_q|$ are the magnitude of voltages of buses p and q, X is the reactance of the line, δ is the difference in phase angles of the voltages of buses p and q. The active power flow P depends largely on the difference in phase angles of the voltages of buses p and q, δ. To control the flow of active power through the line it is necessary to control the phase angle of the voltage at one of the buses. The phase angle of the voltage can be controlled by phase shifting transformers.

3.8 PHASE SHIFTING TRANSFORMERS

The phase shifting transformer injects a quadrature voltage in series with the phase voltage to modify its phase angle. The circuit diagram for one phase is shown in Fig. 3.8.

Fig. 3.8 : Phase shifting transformer for one phase

The voltage added to each phase voltage is displaced by $\pm 90^o$ from it as shown in vector diagram given in Fig. 3.9. It can be seen from the vector diagram that the phase shifting transformer does not cause any appreciable change in magnitude of phase voltages. However, the phase angles are changed

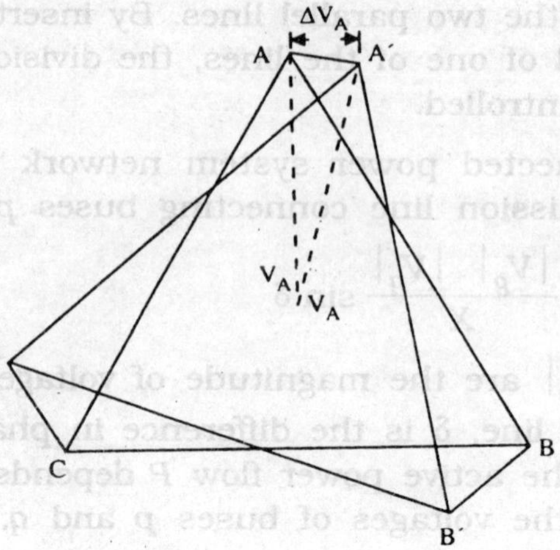

Fig. 3.9 : Vector diagram

and the change in phase angle is approximately proportional to the magnitude of added voltage $|\Delta V|$.

REVIEW QUESTIONS

3.1 Why voltage control is required in a power system?

3.2 Show that the voltage drop in a transmission line largely depends on the reactive power flow through the line. Based on the expression of voltage drop suggest suitable methods of voltage control in power systems.

3.3 Discuss the method of voltage control in power system using tap changing transformers.

3.4 Give the circuit diagram of an on-load tap changer and explain its working.

3.5 Why an underloaded long transmission line requires shunt reactor compensation?

3.6 Why a heavily loaded long transmission line requires shunt capacitor compensation?

3.7 Write a short note on shunt capacitors and reactors.

3.8 Write a short note on series capacitors.

3.9 Describe various types of thyristorised static VAR compensators with their merits and demerits.

3.10 Why phase angle control is required in a power system?

3.11 Discuss phase shifting transformer method of phase angle control in power systems.

Chapter 4

EXCITATION SYSTEMS

The excitation system provides the necessary field current to the rotor winding of the synchronous generator. The amount of excitation depends on the power factor, generator speed and load current.

An excitation system may be a centralised excitation system or individual excitation system. In centralised excitation system two or more exciters feed a bus bar to which the field systems of all alternators of the plant are connected. In individual excitation system each alternator has its separate exciter. A centralised system is cheaper arrangement. However a fault in a centralised excitation system affects all alternators. As such all modern alternators have individual exciters.

The main requirement of an excitation system are reliability under all conditions of service, simplicity of control, ease maintenance, stability and fast transient response. The excitation systems employ Automatic Voltage Regulators (AVR) to control the terminal voltage of the alternator.

The excitation systems can be broadly classified into following types :

1. D.C. excitation system
2. A.C. excitation system.

4.1 D.C. EXCITATION SYSTEM

The d.c. excitation system consists of d.c. generators for supplying field current to the synchronous generator. Fig. 4.1 shows a d.c. excitation system.

The system has two exciters-the main exciter and the pilot exciter. The main exciter is a separately excited d.c. generator and provides the field current to the alternator. The pilot exciter is generally a compound wound self excited d.c. generator and supplies the field current to the main exciter. The pilot exciter output is regulated by an Automatic Voltage Regulator (AVR) to control terminal voltage of the alternator. The current transformer input to the AVR ensures limiting of the alternator current during faults.

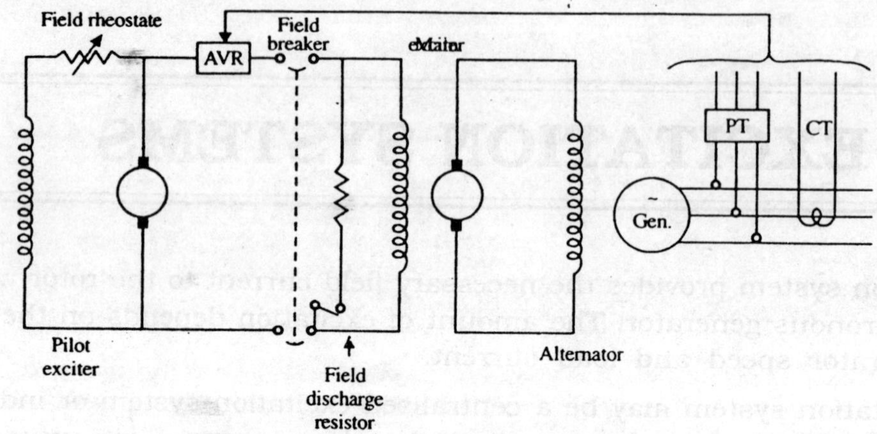

Fig. 4.1 : D.C. Excitation System

The main and pilot exciter can be either driven by the main shaft (directly or through gearing) or separately driven by a motor. Exciters driven from the main shaft preserve the unit system of operation and the excitation is not affected by external disturbances. Therefore the direct driven exciters are preferred. The hydrogenerators run at low speeds therefore the running speed rarely coincides with most economic speed for the particular rating of the exciter. Exciters for small sized turbo-alternators are usually directly coupled to the shaft. For medium and large size turbo-alternators, the exciters are coupled to the main shaft through gears and are usually driven at 1000 rpm. The voltage rating of the main exciter, for both hydrogenerators and turbo-alternators, is around 400V. The exciter capacity is around 0.5% of alternator capacity.

A sudden opening of the excitation circuit may cause a high voltage to be induced in the inductive field winding due to sudden release of energy stored in it. Therefore, as the field breaker opens, it connects a field discharge resistor across the field winding and the energy is dissipated in this resistor.

Troubles in the exciters of turbo-alternators are quite frequent due to the high speed. As such the steam stations are generally equipped with separate motor driven standby exciters.

4.2 A.C. EXCITATION SYSTEM

An a.c. excitation system consists of an a.c. generator and thyristor rectifier bridge directly connected to the alternator shaft. This approach eliminates the commutator, the main alternator field collector rings and some other connections. The main exciter can either be self excited or separately excited. A rotating thyristor excitation system uses a self excited main exciter. The brushless excitation system uses a separately excited main exciter.

4.2.1 Rotating Thyristor Excitation System (Self Excited System)

Fig. 4.2 shows a block diagram of a rotating thyristor excitation system. The portion enclosed by dashed box is the rotating portion of the system.

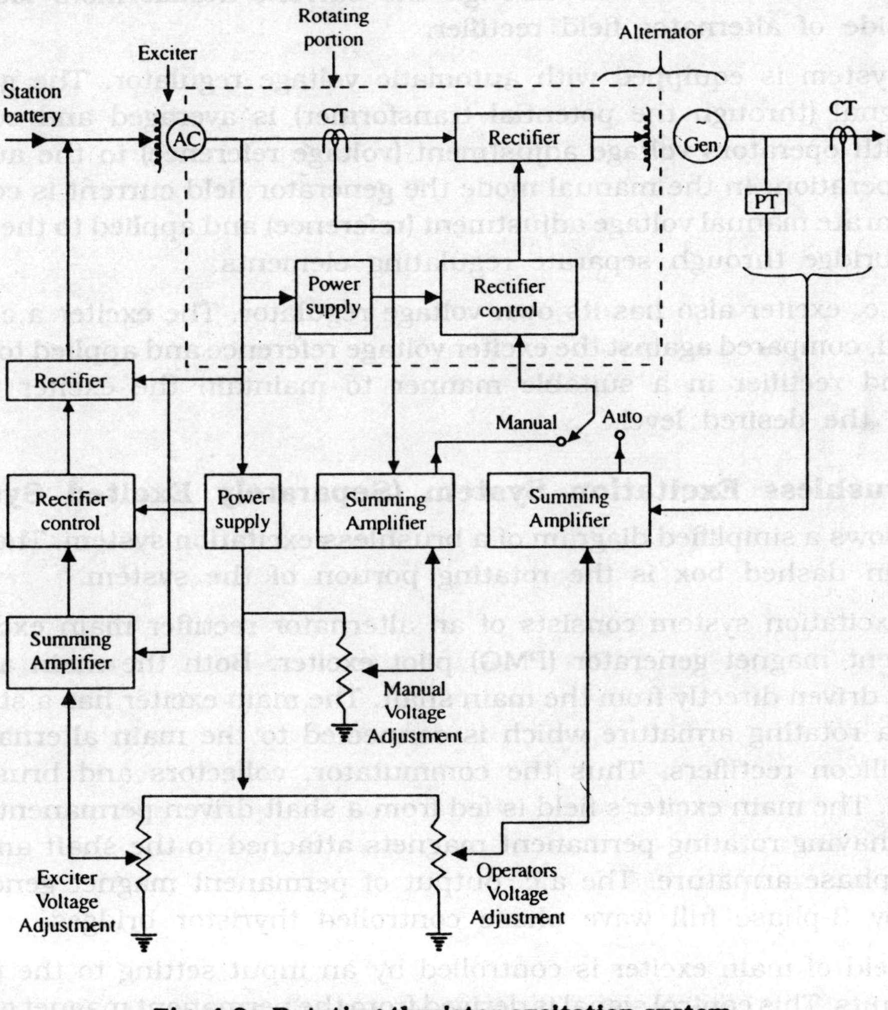

Fig. 4.2 : Rotating thyristor excitation system

The system consists of a.c. exciter having a rotating armature and stationary field winding. The output of the exciter is rectified by a full wave thyristor bridge rectifier circuit and fed to the field winding of the main alternator. The field winding of the exciter is also fed from the exciter output though another rectifier circuit. Exciter voltage builds up due to residual exciter flux. For convenience and to shorten the build up time, station battery supply is also incorporated.

The power supply and rectifier control in rotating portion produce the necessary phase controlled triggering signals according to the d.c. control signal supplied by the voltage regulator circuit summing amplifier. Generator field current measurement is made through the current transformers located on the a.c. side of alternator field rectifier.

The system is equipped with automatic voltage regulator. The generator voltage signal (through the potential transformer) is averaged and compared directly with operators voltage adjustment (voltage reference) in the automatic mode of operation. In the manual mode the generator field current is compared with a separate manual voltage adjustment (reference) and applied to the rotating thyristor bridge through separate regulating elements.

The a.c. exciter also has its own voltage regulator. The exciter a.c. voltage is averaged, compared against the exciter voltage reference and applied to rectifier control and rectifier in a suitable manner to maintain the exciter terminal voltage at the desired level.

4.2.2 Brushless Excitation System (Separately Excited System)

Fig. 4.3 shows a simplified diagram of a brushless excitation system. The portion enclosed in dashed box is the rotating portion of the system.

The excitation system consists of an alternator rectifier main exciter and a permanent magnet generator (PMG) pilot exciter. Both the main and pilot exciter are driven directly from the main shaft. The main exciter has a stationary field and a rotating armature which is connected to the main alternator field through silicon rectifiers. Thus the commutator, collectors and brushes are eliminated. The main exciter's field is fed from a shaft driven permanent magnet generator having rotating permanent magnets attached to the shaft and a stationary 3-phase armature. The a.c. output of permanent magnet generator is rectified by 3-phase full wave phase controlled thyristor bridges.

The field of main exciter is controlled by an input setting to the thyristor gating circuits. This control signal is derived from the permanent magnet generator

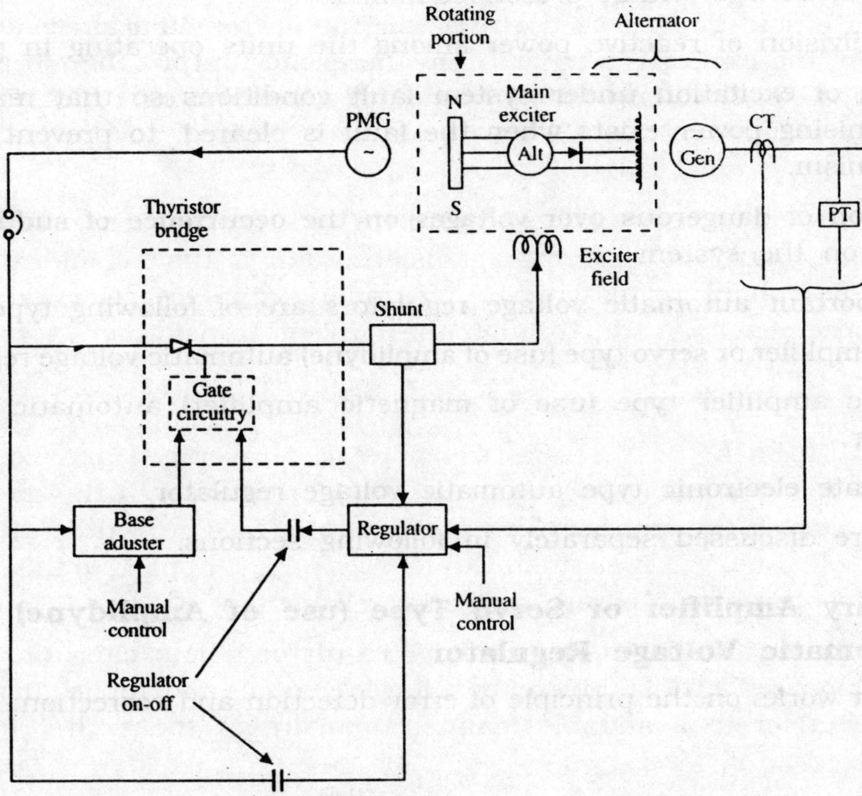

Fig. 4.3 : Brushless excitation system

via a regulated d.c. supply which also serves the regulator logic circuitry. The regulator controls excitation by supplying a buck-boost control signal which adds algebraically to the base setting. The regulator elements also comprise of solid state circuits.

The brushless excitation system eliminates the use of commutator, collector and brushes. It has a short time constant and a response time of less than 0.1 second. The short time constant gives advantage in improved small signal dynamic performance and facilitates the application of supplementary power system stabilizing signals.

4.3 AUTOMATIC VOLTAGE REGULATORS

Every alternator in modern power plants is equipped with an Automatic Voltage

Regulator (AVR) whose functions are :

1. Control of voltage within prescribed limits.
2. Proper division of reactive power among the units operating in parallel.
3. Increase of excitation under system fault conditions so that maximum synchronising power exists when the fault is cleared, to prevent loss of synchronism.
4. Prevention of dangerous over voltages on the occurrence of sudden loss of load on the system.

The important automatic voltage regulators are of following types :

1. Rotary amplifier or servo type (use of amplidyne) automatic voltage regulator.
2. Magnetic amplifier type (use of magnetic amplifier) automatic voltage regulator.
3. Solid State electronic type automatic voltage regulator.

These are discussed separately in following sections.

4.3.1 Rotary Amplifier or Servo Type (use of Amplidyne) Automatic Voltage Regulator

The regulator works on the principle of error detection and correction. Fig. 4.4

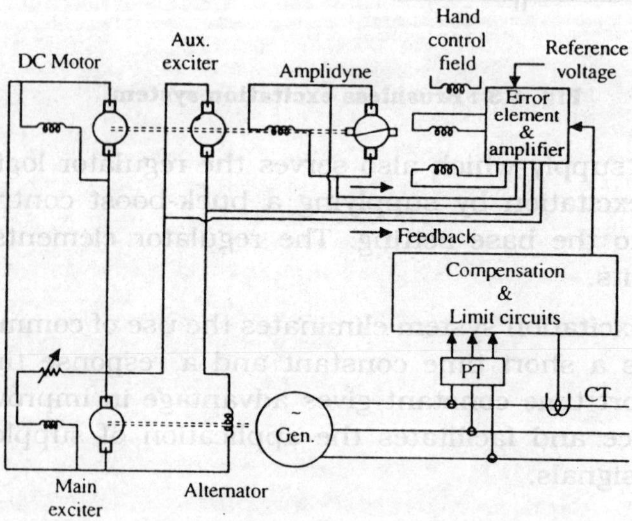

Fig. 4.4 : Servo type regulator using amplidyne

shows a simplified diagram giving the main features of a servo type automatic voltage regulator using amplidyne.

The regulator consists of a direct driven constant voltage main exciter and a motor driven auxiliary exciter whose field is controlled by amplidyne. Both the auxiliary exciter and amplidyne are driven by a d.c. motor fed from main exciter. The outputs of main exciter and auxiliary exciter are connected in series and then fed to the field winding of the alternator.

The alternator 3-phase output voltage is rectified, filtered and compared with the reference voltage. The difference between the actual and the reference is voltage error which is amplified. The amplified error is further suitably amplified through amplidyne (rotary amplifier) and fed to field of the auxiliary exciter connected in series with the main exciter. The voltage generated by the auxiliary exciter is proportional to the voltage error which is added to the voltage generated by the main exciter to correct the error. Thus the amplified error signal controls the excitation of the alternator through buck-boost action.

The several time lags in the circuit necessitate negative feedback for stabilization of system response. The feedback signals are taken from the terminals of amplidyne and auxiliary exciter and fed to the amplifier built with error element.

The automatic voltage regulator has the disadvantage that the response time is high and it requires a large number of rotating machines.

4.3.2 Magnetic Amplifier Type (use of Magnetic Amplifier) Automatic Voltage Regulator

Fig. 4.5 shows a schematic diagram of a magnetic amplifier type automatic voltage regulator.

The alternator has a self excited main exciter whose shunt field provides the base excitation. Base excitation can also be manually controlled by adjusting the motor operated field rheostat. The exciter is also provided with two separately excited control fields which are energised from the power magnetic amplifier. The power magnetic amplifier feeds either the buck or boost control field to lower or raise the excitation voltage required to maintain fixed terminal voltage of the alternator.

The reference element, energised from a separate a.c. supply, produces a reference quantity used as a basis of comparison. The compensation circuits provide the reactive drop compensation as required by the system and limit circuits limit the alternator voltage and current within prescribed limits.

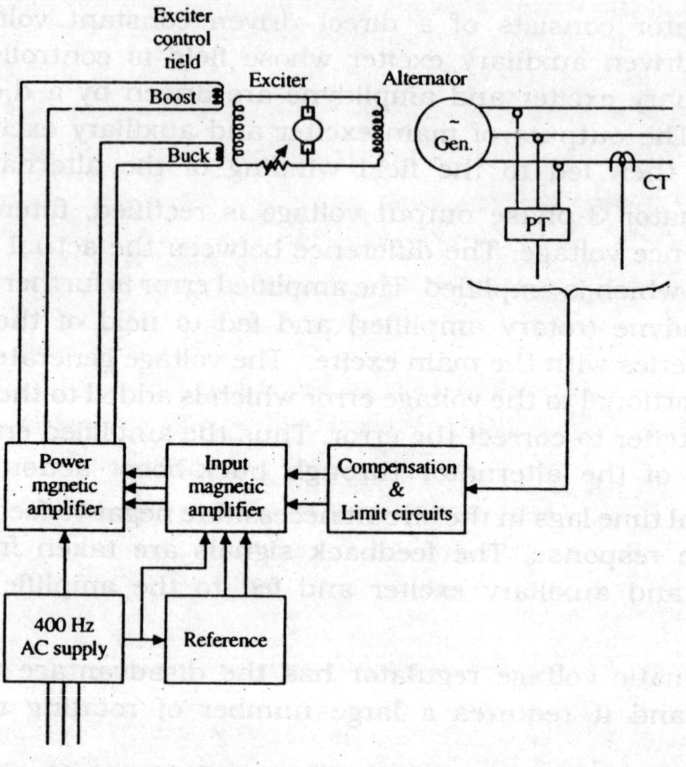

Fig. 4.5 : Magnetic amplifier type automatic voltage regulator

The alternator terminal voltage, modified by compensation and limit circuits, is supplied to input magnetic amplifier where it is also compared with the reference. The input magnetic amplifier is a two stage push pull amplifier. Push pull circuitry allows output polarity reversal as a function of the polarity of control signal to achieve a buck or boost action. The amplified error signal produced by input magnetic amplifier is fed to a power magnetic amplifier which has two units; one unit is polarised to respond a boost error signal and the other to a buck error signal. The two amplified error signals drive exciter control field windings in such a manner that the generated exciter voltage produces desired constant terminal voltage of the alternator.

The high frequency a.c. supply of 400 Hz required for the regulating system is obtained from a separate permanent magnet motor generator set. The high frequency a.c. supply ensures that the delay of the regulating system is negligible as compared to the delay of the exciter and alternator. Another advantage is that the size of the reactors become small. The regulator is costlier as compared with the electronic automatic voltage regulator.

4.3.3 Solid State (Electronic) type Automatic Voltage Regulator

The block diagram of the Solid State (electronic) type automatic voltage regulator is shown in Fig. 4.6.

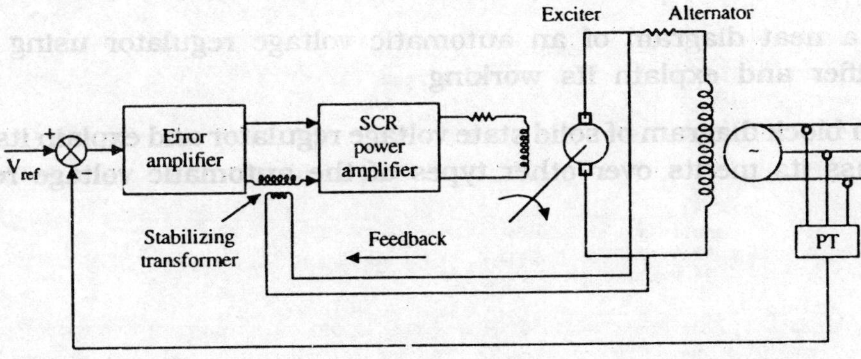

Fig. 4.6 : Solid State (electronic) regulator

The terminal voltage of the alternator obtained through potential transformer is rectified, compared with reference and then amplified using error amplifier and power amplifier stages. The amplified error is fed into the exciter field which produces field voltage for alternator such that the alternator terminal voltage remains constant.

The stabilizing transformer provides feedback of exciter voltage to improve dynamic response. The advantages of electronic automatic voltage regulators are accuracy of control, high speed of response, high reliability and minimum maintenance. Earlier the electronic regulators used vacuum and gas tubes but now a days solid state devices such as transistors, integrated circuits and SCRs are used. The solid state devices consume less power and provide high reliability.

REVIEW QUESTIONS

4.1 What is the purpose of excitation system? On which factors the excitation depends? What are the main requirements of excitation systems?

4.2 Distinguish between centralised and individual excitation systems. Give relative merits and demerits of the two types of the excitation systems.

4.3 Draw and describe a D.C. excitation system.

4.4 Draw and describe a separately excited A.C. excitation system.

4.5 Draw and describe a self excited A.C. excitation system.

4.6 Give a neat diagram of an automatic voltage regulator using amplidyne and explain its working.

4.7 Give a neat diagram of an automatic voltage regulator using magnetic amplifier and explain its working.

4.8 Give a block diagram of solid state voltage regulator and explain its working. Discuss its merits over other types of the automatic voltage regulators.

Chapter 5

POWER SYSTEM STABILITY AND SECURITY

An interconnected power system has several generators and many loads. For parallel operation of the generators all the generators must run at same speed *i.e.*, they should run in synchronism. The power system is never static therefore the disturbances such as changes in load or the faults etc. are capable to disturb the synchronous operation of various generators of the system. The power system stability refers to the problem of synchronous operation of various machines of power system following a disturbance.

5.1 MEANING OF POWER SYSTEM STABILITY

The stability of a physical system is referred as its capability to return to the original or a new equilibrium state on the occurrence of a disturbance. During transient period, following the disturbance, the system state may not be in equilibrium but as time passes and tends to infinity the system achieves an equilibrium state if the system is stable. In the equilibrium state the physical variables do not change with time.

A power system has a number of synchronous machines operating in parallel. The voltage in synchronous machines is generated by the flux produced by field windings of the machines therefore the phase difference between the generated voltages of any two machines is the same as the electrical angle between the corresponding machine rotors (poles). When the machines are running with synchronism, the rotor angles of all the synchronous machines with reference to a synchronously rotating reference axis do not change with time denoting that the power system is in equilibrium state. If the machines are not running with synchronism, a few machines may be running faster than the others and the angular position of their rotor relative to the other machines will continue to advance resulting in continuous advancement of their generated voltage phase angle relative to the voltage angle of slower machines. This denotes that the system is not in equilibrium state. Therefore, the power system operates in equilibrium state if the various synchronous machines in the system are running in synchronism or in step with each other.

The stability of an interconnected power system is its ability to return to equilibrium state, *i.e.*, a state in which all the synchronous machines are running with synchronism, after having been subjected to some form of disturbance. The disturbance may be as simple as very small slow change in loads or as large or complex as sudden change in loads, loss of generators, transmission facilities etc. The precise definition of stability as published by American Institute of Electrical Engineers is as follows :

Stability when used with reference to the power system, is that attribute of the system, or part of the system, which enables it to develop restoring forces between the elements thereof, equal to or grater than the disturbing forces so as to restore a state of equilibrium between the elements.

5.2 STEADY STATE, TRANSIENT AND DYNAMIC STABILITY

The power system stability can be classified into steady state stability, transient stability and dynamic stability according to the magnitude and duration of disturbance and time frame of study. The steady state, transient and dynamic stability are defined separately in following sections.

5.2.1 Steady State Stability

A power system operating state has steady state stability if after a small slow disturbance it can regain and maintain synchronism at rated frequency. The normal load variations or changes come in the category of small slow disturbances.

5.2.2 Transient Stability

A power system operating state has transient stability if, after a large sudden disturbance, it can regain and maintain synchronism at rated frequency. The large sudden disturbances are sudden change in loads, loss of generators, excitations, transmission facilities and switching operations and faults etc.

The disturbances usually considered in transient stability studies are the most severe ones such as a short circuit on the transmission lines, buses or at transformer terminals. A fault on a heavily loaded line which requires opening the line to clear the fault is usually of greatest concern.

The transient stability phenomenon is a very fast one therefore usually the transient stability studies are restricted upto one second or fraction of it. The action of voltage regulators (which control induced emf) and turbine governors (which govern mechanical input) is not included in transient stability studies because these devices are too slow to act during this interval. Therefore, mechanical input and the induced voltage are assumed constant in the transient stability studies and if the machines of the power system do not loose synchronism within one second then it is assumed that the system is stable.

As discussed earlier, the synchronism in a power system is related with synchronous machine rotor angles. If the individual machine rotor angles with reference to a synchronously rotating axis are fixed and not changing with time, the power system is said to be operating in synchronism. The transient stability may also be defined as follows :

For one synchronous machine connected to infinite bus

An infinite bus is one whose voltage, magnitude as well as phase angle, and frequency are constant irrespective of loadings and disturbances. The infinite bus can be taken as reference bus.

If a synchronous machine operating in steady state equilibrium is subjected to a disturbance of any kind which results in deviations (oscillations) of the machine rotor angle from the (synchronously rotating) reference axis, then the machine is called stable from transient stability viewpoint if the rotor ultimately reaches a new stable equilibrium position. However, to ensure the transient stability it is sufficient to ensure that during the period of study (usually one second) the deviations of rotor angles do not cross the limit (usually 180°).

For a multimachine system

If the individual machines in a multimachine system are operating in steady state equilibrium and a disturbance of any kind is imposed on the system, then the system is called stable from transient stability view point if each machine rotor oscillates around and ultimately comes to rest at a new stable equilibrium point. However, to ensure the transient stability it is sufficient to ensure that for all pairs of machines the rotor angle of one machine with reference to the other do not cross the limit (usually 180°) within the period of study (usually one second).

5.2.3 Dynamic Stability

A power system operating state has dynamic stability if, after a large sudden disturbance, it can regain and maintain synchronism at rated frequency when the action of voltage regulators and turbine governors is also included. The large sudden disturbances are sudden change in loads, loss of generators, excitations, transmission facilities and switching operations and faults etc.

The dynamic stability study is similar to transient stability study except that the action of voltage regulator and governor is included in dynamic stability study. In dynamic stability studies the system is analysed for a period of 4-10 seconds following a large disturbance such as a short circuit or loss of generation or loss of load etc.

5.3 POWER LIMITS OF TRANSMISSION LINES

The maximum power which can be transmitted through a transmission line is also limited due to the stability. The stability limit is defined as the maximum power which can flow through the line without causing loss of stability. A transmission line has steady state stability limit as well as transient stability limit. These limits are defined as follows.

The steady state stability limit is the maximum possible flow of power through the transmission line without loss of stability, when the power is increased very slowly.

The transient stability limit is the maximum possible flow of power without loss of stability, when the instability may be caused by a specified large sudden disturbance.

5.3.1 Steady State Stability Limit of a Transmission Line

Consider a simple power system, shown in Fig. 5.1, consisting of a synchronous

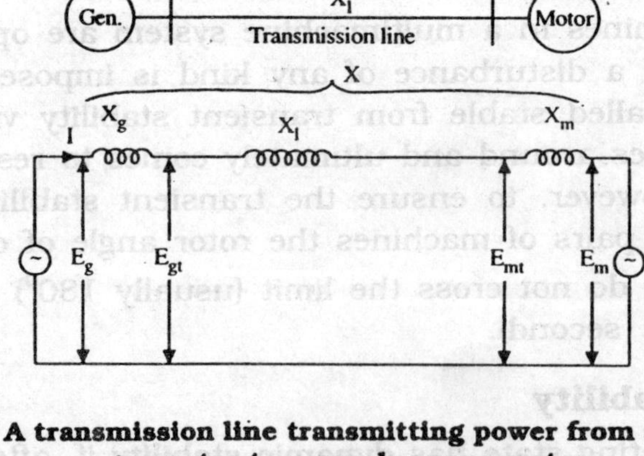

Fig. 5.1 : A transmission line transmitting power from synchronous generator to a synchronous motor

generator supplying power to a synchronous motor over a transmission line having reactance X_l.

Each of the synchronous machines may be represented by a constant voltage source in series with a constant reactance. Thus the generator is represented by E_g and X_g, and the motor by E_m and X_m. Upon combining the machine reactances and the line reactance into a single reactance we have an electric circuit consisting of two constant voltage sources, E_g and E_m, connected through reactance $X = X_g + X_l + X_m$ as shown in Fig. 5.2.

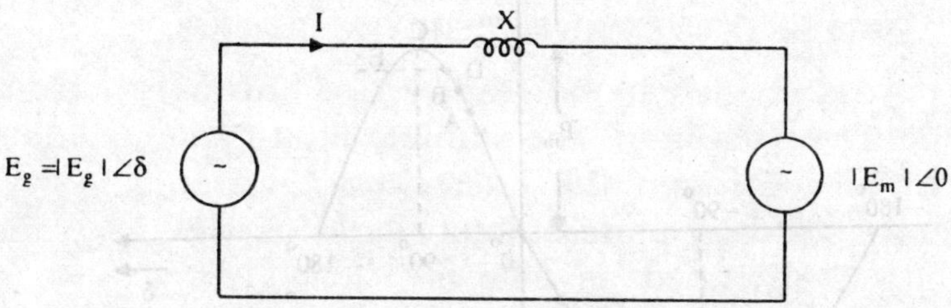

Fig. 5.2 : Equivalent circuit

The power flow, P, through the transmission line is given by :

$$P = \text{Re}\,[E_g I^*] \qquad \text{...(5.1)}$$

where Re means "real part of". Taking $E_g = |E_g| \underline{|\delta}$ and $E_m = |E_m| \underline{|0}$ we have

$$I = \frac{|E_g| \underline{|\delta} - |E_m| \underline{|0}}{jX} = \frac{|E_g| \underline{|\delta} - |E_m| \underline{|0}}{X \underline{|90^\circ}} \qquad \text{...(5.2)}$$

From Eqs. (5.1) and (5.2)

$$P = \text{Re}\left[|E_g| \underline{|\delta} \left[\frac{|E_g| \underline{|\delta} - |E_m| \underline{|0}}{X \underline{|90^\circ}} \right]^* \right]$$

$$= \text{Re}\left[|E_g| \underline{|\delta} \left[\frac{|E_g| \underline{|-\delta} - |E_m| \underline{|-0}}{X \underline{|-90^\circ}} \right] \right]$$

$$= \text{Re}\left[|E_g| \underline{|\delta} \left[\frac{|E_g|}{X} \underline{|90-\delta} - \frac{|E_m|}{X} \underline{|90} \right] \right]$$

$$= \text{Re}\left[\frac{|E_g|^2}{X} \underline{|90} - \frac{|E_g|\;|E_m|}{X} \underline{|90+\delta} \right]$$

$$= -\frac{|E_g|\ |E_m|}{X} \cos(90 + \delta)$$

$$= \frac{|E_g|\ |E_m|}{X} \sin \delta \qquad ...(5.3)$$

The power flow P varies with the phase angle difference δ as shown in Fig. 5.3.

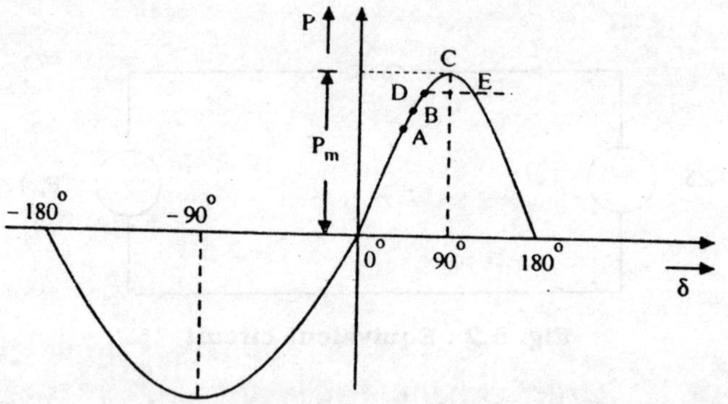

Fig. 5.3 : Power angle curve of the system

Since the generator and motor voltages are generated by the flux produced by the field windings of the machines, their phase difference is the same as the electrical angle between the machine rotors. Suppose that the system is operating in the steady state at point A as shown in Fig. 5.3. The mechanical input of the generator and the mechanical output of the motor will be equal to the electrical power P, if losses are neglected. Now suppose that a small increment of shaft load is added to the motor. Just after the increment the angular position of the rotor remains unchanged therefore the motor mechanical output is more than its electrical input. Therefore, there is a net retarding torque on the motor causing its speed to decrease temporarily. As a result of the decrease in motor speed, δ increases, and consequently the power input increases until finally the input and output are again in equilibrium. Steady operation is attained at a new operating point, say at point B, higher than point A on the power angle curve.

Suppose that the motor output is increased gradually until the point C of maximum power $P_m = \frac{|E_g|\ |E_m|}{X}$ is reached. If now additional increment of load is put on the motor, the displacement angle δ will increase as before, but as it does so there will be no increase in input. Instead there will be a decrease in input, further increasing the difference between output and input, and retarding the motor more rapidly. The motor will pull out of step. Therefore $P_m = \frac{|E_g| \; |E_m|}{X}$ is the steady state stability limit of the system. If generator and motor reactances are neglected, the steady state stability limit of the transmission line is given by

$$P_m = \frac{|V_s| \; |V_r|}{X_l}$$

where V_s and V_r are the sending end and receiving end voltages respectively.

5.3.2 Transient Stability Limit of a Transmission Line

Consider the simple system consisting of a generator, transmission line and motor as shown in Figs. 5.1 and 5.2 discussed earlier. The power flow through the transmission line is given by Eq. (5.3). The power angle curve of the system is shown in Fig. 5.3. If a large increment of load on the motor is added suddenly, instead of gradually, the motor may fall out of step even though the new load does not exceed the steady state limit. The reason is as follows.

Let the system be operating with certain loading, say at operating point *A* shown in Fig. 5.3. When the large increment of load is added suddenly to the motor shaft, say corresponding to operating point *D*, the mechanical power output of the motor greatly exceeds the electrical power input, and the deficiency of input is supplied by decrease of kinetic energy. The motor slows down resulting in an increase of displacement angle δ and a consequent input. In accordance with the assumption that the new load does not exceed the steady state stability limit, δ increases to the proper value for steady state operation *i.e.*, upto operating point *D*. At this operating point the motor input equals the output and the retarding torque vanishes. When this value of δ is reached, however, the motor is running too slowly. Its angular momentum prevents its speed from suddenly increasing to the normal value. Hence it continues to run too slowly, and the angle δ increases beyond the proper value *i.e.*, beyond point *D*. After the angle has passed this value, the motor input exceeds the output, and the net torque is now accelerating torque. The speed of the motor increases and may approach to normal speed. Before normal speed is regained, however, the angle δ may have increased to such an extent that the operating point on the power angle curve not only goes over the hump, the operating point *C*, but also goes so far over it that the motor input decreases to a value less than the output, which happens when operating point crosses point *E*. If this happens, the net torque changes from an accelerating torque to a retarding torque. The speed, which is still below normal, now decreases again, and continues to decrease. The synchronism is therefore definitely lost. In other words, the system is unstable.

If, however, the sudden increment in load is not too great, the motor will regain its normal speed before the angle δ becomes too great *i.e.*, before operating point *E*. In this situation, at the instant when normal speed is regained the net torque is still an accelerating torque and causes the motor speed to continue to increase and thus to become greater than normal. The displacement angle then decreases and again approaches its proper value, point *D*. Again it overshoots on account of inertia. The rotor of the motor thus oscillates about the new steady-state angular position. The oscillations finally die out because of damping torques such as due to damper windings etc. which have been neglected in this elementary analysis. A damped oscillatory motion characterizes a stable system.

With a given sudden increment in load, there is a definite upper limit to the load which the transmission line will carry without pulling out of step. This is the transient stability limit of the transmission line for the given conditions. The transient stability limit is always below the steady state stability limit and therefore very important. The transient stability limit may have many different values, depending upon the nature and magnitude of the disturbance. Studies have shown that the power flows corresponding to δ upto 30° may result in stable operation for usual disturbances.

5.4 REPRESENTATION OF SYNCHRONOUS MACHINES

For a salient pole machine the per phase induced emf-terminal voltage equation under steady state condition is

$$E = V + jX_d I_d + jX_q I_q \quad \ldots(5.4)$$

where, E = induced emf per phase

V = terminal voltage per phase

X_d = direct axis reactance of the machine

X_q = quadrature axis reactance of the machine

I_d = direct axis component of stator current

I_q = quadrature axis component of stator current

$I = I_d + I_q$ = stator current

Neglecting saliency for salient pole machines, we have

$$X_d = X_q = X_s = \text{synchronous reactance}$$

the Eq. (5.4) becomes

$$E = V + jX_s\, I_d + jX_s\, I_q$$

$$= V + jX_s\,(I_d + I_q)$$

or

$$E = V + jX_s\, I \qquad \text{...(5.5)}$$

The machine model corresponding to Eq. (5.5) is shown in Fig. 5.4 which also applies to cylindrical rotor machine because for such machine $X_d = X_q = X_s =$ synchronous reactance.

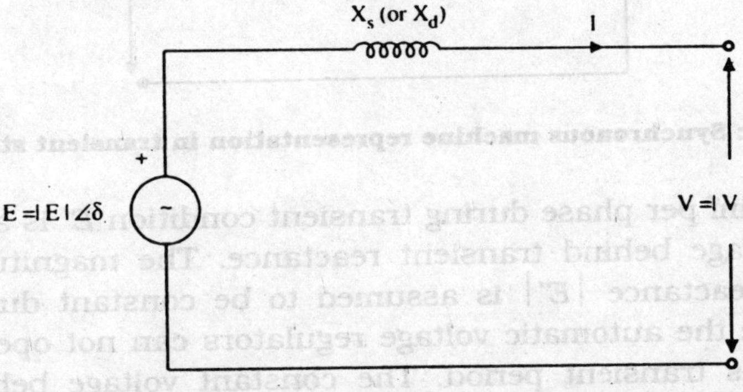

Fig. 5.4 : Synchronous machine representation in steady state

Fig. 5.4 gives representation of synchronous machine under steady state conditions. The model is used for steady state stability studies and balanced three phase short circuit studies. The model is approximate for salient pole machines for which exact model is given by Eq. (5.4). The model is exact for cylindrical rotor machines.

Under transient conditions X_d becomes X_d' where $X_d' \ll X_d$. However X_q remains almost unaffected therefore $X_q' \approx X_q$. It is found that $X_d' < X_q$ but the difference is less than that of between X_d and X_q. The Eq. (5.4) during transient conditions modifies to

$$E' = V + jX_d'\, I_d + jX_q\, I_q \qquad \text{...(5.6)}$$

It is fairly valid to assume that $X_d' = X_q$. Therefore Eq. (5.6) now becomes

$$E' = V + jX_d' I_d + jX_d' I_q$$

$$= V + jX_d' (I_d + I_q)$$

or
$$E' = V + jX_d' I \qquad \text{...(5.7)}$$

The machine model corresponding to Eq. (5.7) is drawn in Fig. 5.5 which also applies to a cylindrical rotor machine where $X_d' = X_q' = X_s'$ (transient synchronous reactance)

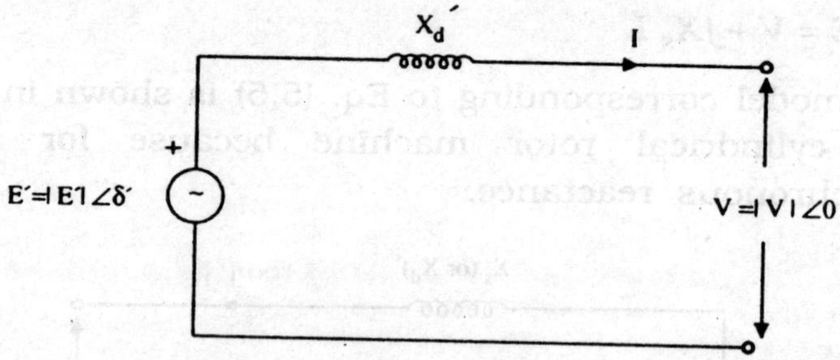

Fig. 5.5 : Synchronous machine representation in transient state

The induced emf per phase during transient condition E' is also commonly referred to as voltage behind transient reactance. The magnitude of voltage behind transient reactance $|E'|$ is assumed to be constant during transient conditions because the automatic voltage regulators can not operate in a very short time such as transient period. The constant voltage behind transient reactance $|E'|$ and initial value of δ' are determined from Eq. (5.7) where the values of V and I are taken as the pretransient values. During the transient period the magnitude $|E'|$ is held constant while the angle δ' varies which is considered as the angle between the rotor position and the terminal voltage V, and is determined from the dynamics of synchronous machine (using inertia constant and swing equation).

Example 5.1. Fig. 5.6 shows a generator transformer unit feeding an infinite bus bar through a transmission line. At the middle of the transmission line a 3-phase inductor of reactance 0.5 pu per phase is connected. The generator e.m.f. behind synchronous reactance is 1.1 pu and the voltage of infinite bus is 1 pu. Calculate (*a*) transfer reactance and steady state power limit with inductor switch open, (*b*) transfer reactance and steady state power limit with inductor switch closed, (*c*) transfer reactance and steady state power limit with inductor replaced by a capacitor of the same pu reactance, and (*d*) transfer reactance and steady state power limit if, instead of shunt capacitor, a series capacitor of the same per unit reactance is connected in series with the line at the same location.

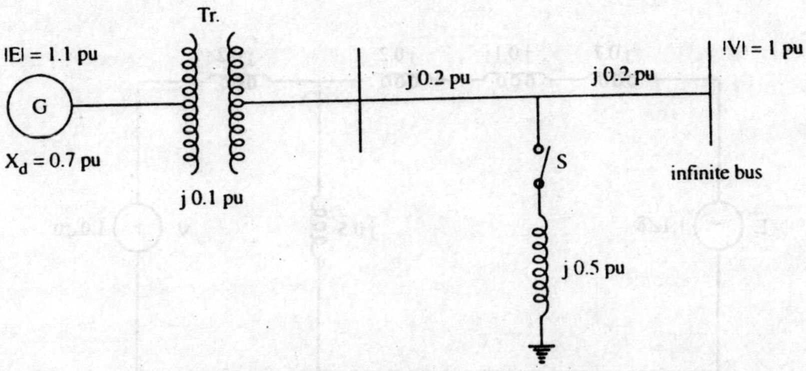

Fig. 5.6 : A generator transformer unit feeding an infinite bus through a transmission line

Solution :

(*a*) **When switch S is open :** The transfer reactance is the total series reactance between the generator e.m.f. and the infinite bus. The equivalent circuit of the system with switch *S* open is shown in Fig. 5.7.

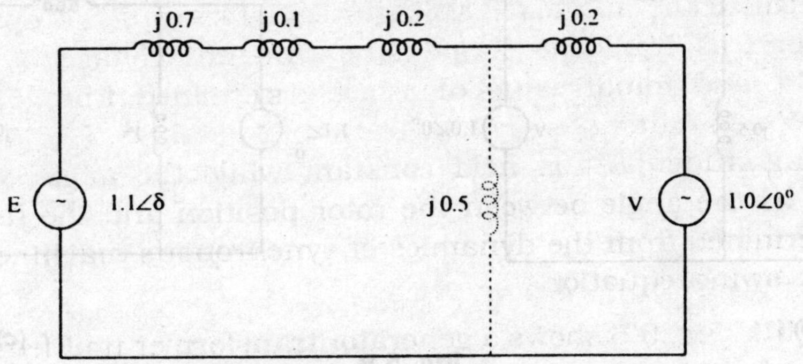

Fig. 5.7 : Equivalent circuit with switch S open

From the Fig. 5.7 the transfer reactance

$$X = 0.7 + 0.1 + 0.2 + 0.2 = 1.2 \text{ pu}$$

Steady state power limit

$$P_m = \frac{|E|\ |V|}{X} = \frac{1.1 \times 1}{1.2} = 0.91667 \text{ pu.}$$

(*b*) **When switch S is closed :** With the switch *S* closed, the equivalent circuit of the system is developed in Figs. 5.8 (*a*) to 5.8 (*c*). The series reactances

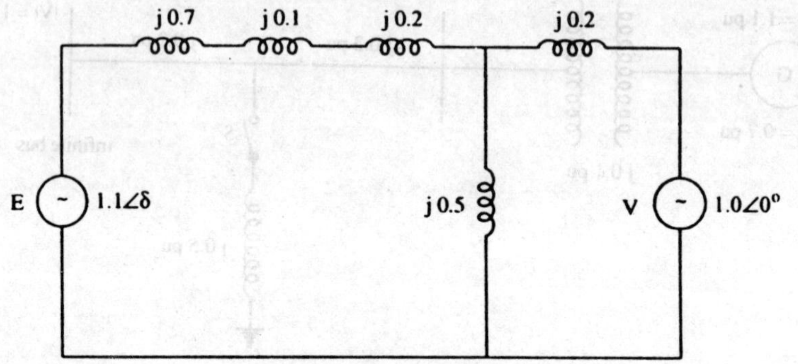

Fig. 5.8 (*a*)

in Fig. 5.8 (*a*) are combined together in Fig. 5.8 (*b*) and the star connected reactances of Fig. 5.8 (*b*) are converted into equivalent delta in Fig. 5.8 (*c*).

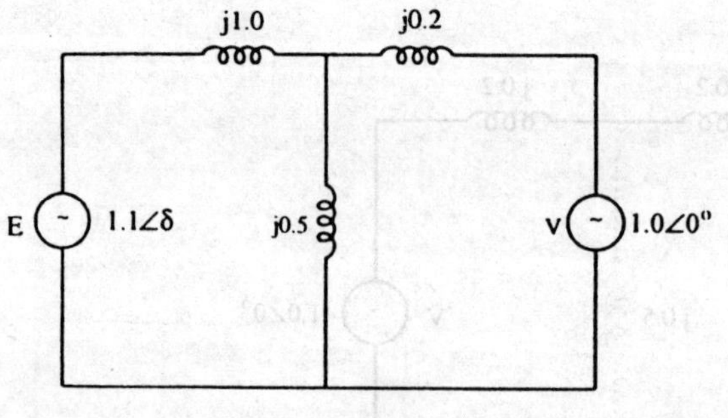

(*b*)

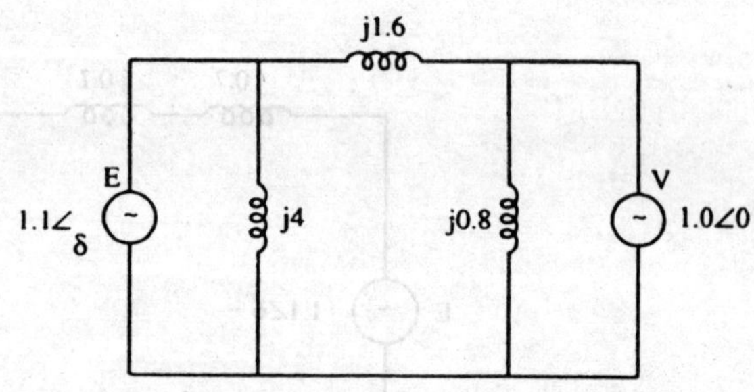

(*c*)

Fig. 5.8

From Fig. 5.8 (*c*) the transfer reactance between the generator e.m.f. and the infinite bus

$$X = 1.6 \text{ pu.}$$

Steady state power limit

$$P_m = \frac{|E|\ |V|}{X} = \frac{1.1 \times 1}{1.6} = 0.6875 \text{ pu}$$

(The shunt reactances across the generator e.m.f. and infinite bus do not effect the power transfer from the generator bus to the infinite bus as these are across constant sources. The active power P_m from generator e.m.f. bus is fully transferred to the infinite bus as the shunt reactances do not consume any active power.)

(c) **When the inductive reactor is replaced by a capacitor of value 0.5 pu :** The equivalent circuit of the system is developed in Figs. 5.9 (*a*)

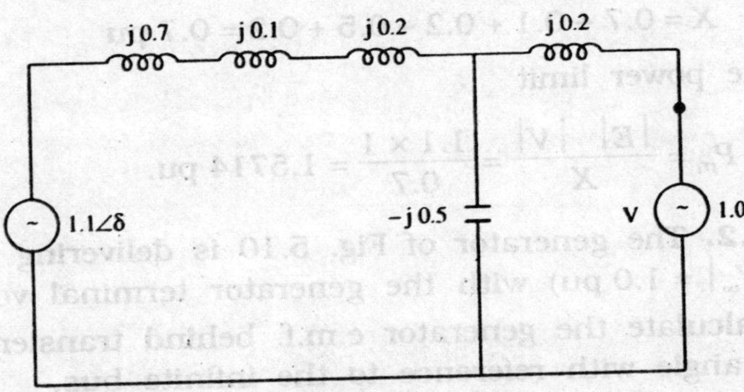

Fig. 5.9 (*a*)

to 5.9 (*c*). The series reactances in Fig. 5.9 (*a*) are combined together in Fig. 5.9 (*b*) and the star connected reactances of Fig. 5.9 (*b*) are converted into equivalent delta in Fig. 5.9 (*c*).

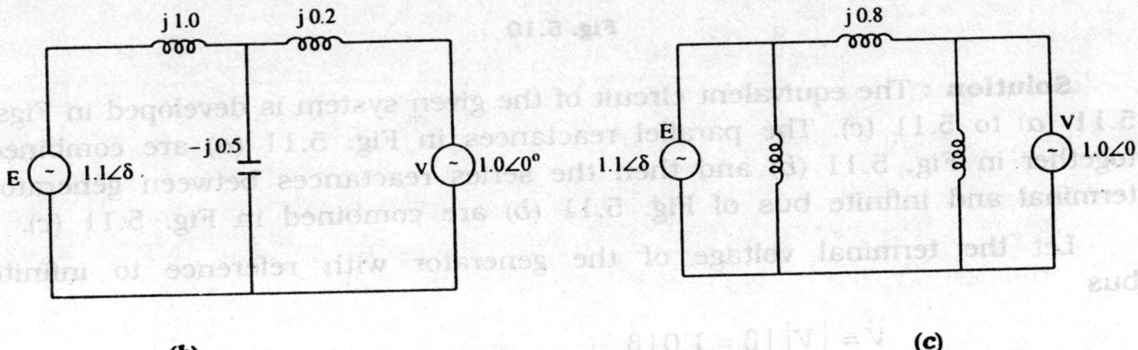

Fig. 5.9

From Fig. 5.9 (*c*) the transfer reactance between the generator e.m.f. and the infinite bus

$$X = 0.8 \text{ pu.}$$

Steady state power limit

$$P_m = \frac{|E|\ |V|}{X} = \frac{1.1 \times 1}{0.8} = 1.375 \text{ pu.}$$

(*d*) **When the shunt capacitor is replaced by a series capacitor :** From the Fig. 5.7 the transfer reactance with shunt inductor replaced by series capacitor of 0.5 pu is

$$X = 0.7 + 0.1 + 0.2 - 0.5 + 0.2 = 0.7 \text{ pu}$$

Steady state power limit

$$P_m = \frac{|E|\ |V|}{X} = \frac{1.1 \times 1}{0.7} = 1.5714 \text{ pu.}$$

Example 5.2. The generator of Fig. 5.10 is delivering 1.0 pu power to infinite bus ($|V_\infty| = 1.0$ pu) with the generator terminal voltage magnitude $|V| = 1.0$ pu. Calculate the generator e.m.f. behind transient reactance and generator rotor angle with reference to the infinite bus.

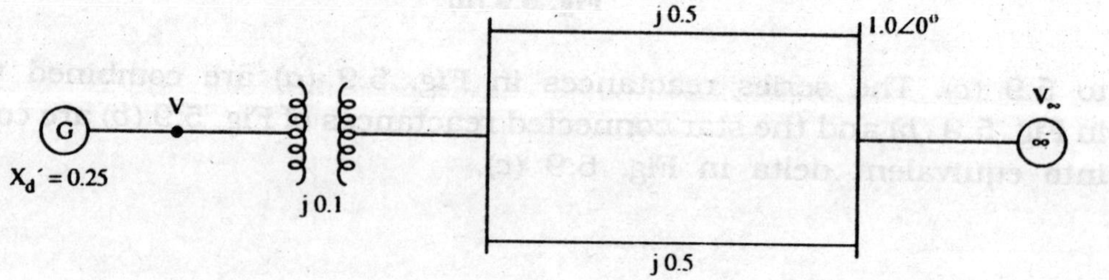

Fig. 5.10

Solution : The equivalent circuit of the given system is developed in Figs. 5.11 (*a*) to 5.11 (*c*). The parallel reactances in Fig. 5.11 (*a*) are combined together in Fig. 5.11 (*b*) and then the series reactances between generator terminal and infinite bus of Fig. 5.11 (*b*) are combined in Fig. 5.11 (*c*).

Let the terminal voltage of the generator with reference to infinite bus

$$V = |V| \angle \beta = 1.0 \angle \beta$$

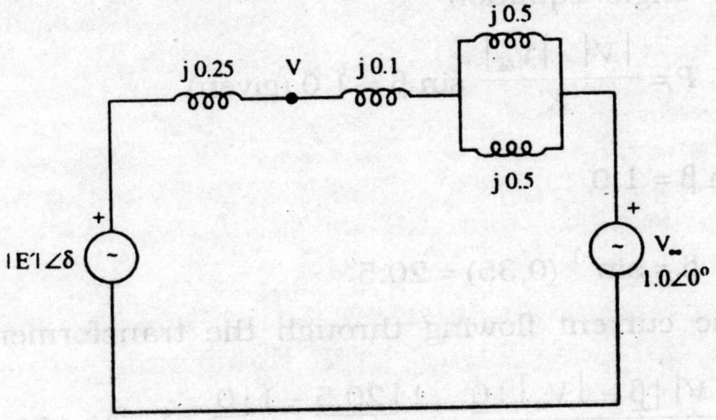

Fig. 5.11 (*a*)

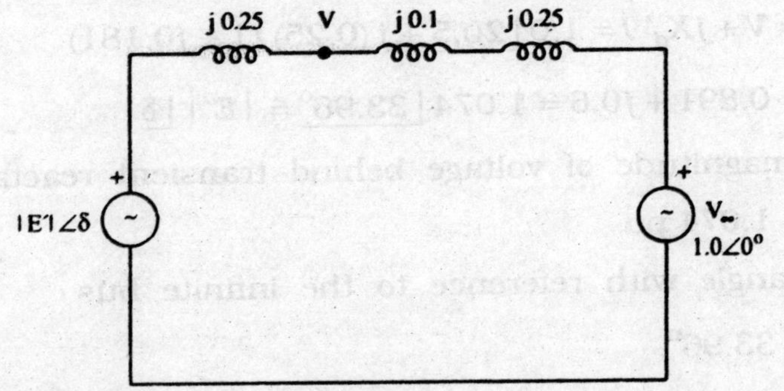

Fig. 5.11 (*b*)

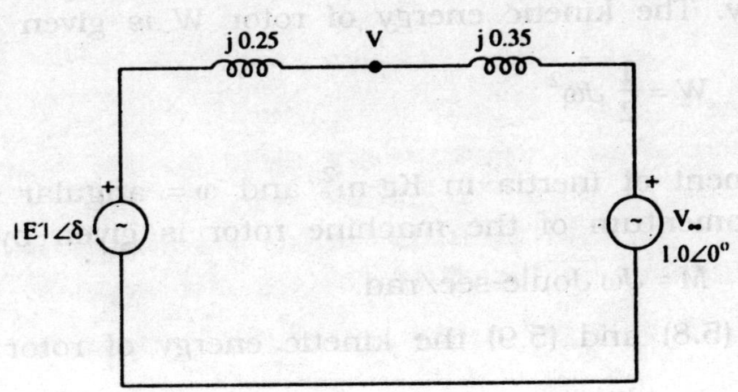

Fig. 5.11 (*c*)

From power angle equation

$$P = \frac{|V|\ |V_\infty|}{X} \sin\beta = 1.0 \text{ (given)}$$

or $$\frac{1 \times 1}{(0.35)} \sin\beta = 1.0$$

or $$\beta = \sin^{-1}(0.35) = 20.5^\circ$$

Therefore the current flowing through the transformer

$$I = \frac{|V| \angle\beta - |V_\infty| \angle 0}{jX} = \frac{1\angle 20.5 - 1\angle 0}{j0.35} = 1 + j0.181 = 1.016\angle 10.3^\circ$$

$= \text{generator current}$

Voltage behind transient reactance

$$E' = V + jX_d' I = 1.0\angle 20.5 + j\,(0.25)\,(1 + j0.181)$$

$$= 0.891 + j0.6 = 1.074\angle 33.96^\circ = |E'| \angle\delta$$

Therefore magnitude of voltage behind transient reactance

$$|E'| = 1.074 \text{ pu}$$

and the rotor angle with reference to the infinite bus

$$\delta = 33.96^\circ.$$

5.5 INERTIA CONSTANT

During the transient period the rotor speed undergo changes which is governed by the inertia of the rotor and amount of exchange of its kinetic energy with electrical energy. The kinetic energy of rotor W is given by

$$W = \frac{1}{2} J\omega^2 \qquad \text{...(5.8)}$$

where J = moment of inertia in Kg-m^2 and ω = angular speed in rad/sec. The angular momentum of the machine rotor is given by

$$M = J\omega \text{ Joule-sec/rad.} \qquad \text{...(5.9)}$$

From Eqs. (5.8) and (5.9) the kinetic energy of rotor is given by

$$W = \frac{1}{2} M\omega \qquad \text{...(5.10)}$$

The inertia constant H is defined as the energy stored in rotor Megajoules per MVA rating at synchronous speed. Therefore if MVA rating of the machine is G then

$$H = \frac{\text{Stored energy in Megajoules}}{\text{Rating in MVA}} = \frac{W}{G} \quad \text{...(5.11)}$$

From Eqs. (5.8), (5.10) and (5.11) we have

$$W = \frac{1}{2} J\omega^2 = \frac{1}{2} M\omega = GH$$

so $$GH = \frac{1}{2} M\omega = \frac{1}{2} M(2\pi f) \quad \text{(because } \omega = 2\pi f\text{)}$$

or $$M = \frac{GH}{\pi f} \text{ MJ-sec/radian}$$

or $$M = \frac{GH}{180 f} \text{ MJ-sec/electrical-degree} \quad \text{...(5.12)}$$

During transient period angular speed ω is not constant but the deviations of it from synchronous speed are usually not large. Therefore it may be assumed that the angular speed ω of the synchronous machines is constant and equal to the synchronous speed during transient period. At this speed the frequency f is equal to the rated frequency. Under the assumption of constant angular speed ω the kinetic energy $W = \frac{1}{2} J\omega^2$ and hence value of inertia constant H and angular momentum M, given by Eqs. (5.11) and (5.12), are also constant. The angular momentum M is also commonly called as inertia constant but its unit is Megajoule-sec per electrical degree whereas inertia constant H is in per unit.

The inertia constant H is widely used by manufacturers. The advantage of using H from manufacturers viewpoint is that its value is fairly constant over a wide range of MVA rating of each class of machine. The typical values of H for turbo alternators range between 3 – 10 MJ/MVA and for waterwheel alternators range between 2 – 4 MJ/MVA. Synchronous motor has inertia constant H about 2.0 MJ/MVA and synchronous condenser in the range 1 – 1.25 MJ/MVA.

When several machines at one point, or at nearby, are considered as a single equivalent machine then

Total Kinetic energy = kinetic energy of equivalent machine

= sum of kinetic energy of each machine

so $$H_{eq}\, G_{eq} = H_1\, G_1 + H_2\, G_2 + \ldots + H_n\, G_n$$

or $$H_{eq}\, G_{base} = H_1\, G_1 + H_2\, G_2 + \ldots + H_n\, G_n$$

where $G_{eq} = G_{base}$ = base MVA.

therefore $$H_{eq} = \frac{H_1\, G_1}{G_{base}} + \frac{H_2\, G_2}{G_{base}} + \ldots + \frac{H_n\, G_n}{G_{base}} \qquad \ldots(5.13)$$

Also, by using Eq. (5.12),

$$M_{eq} = \frac{G_{base}\, H_{eq}}{180f} = \frac{H_1\, G_1}{180f} + \frac{H_2\, G_2}{180f} + \ldots + \frac{H_n\, G_n}{180f}$$

or $$M_{eq} = M_1 + M_2 + \ldots + M_n \qquad \ldots(5.14)$$

Example 5.3. A 50 Hz, 4 pole, turbo generator rated at 20 MVA, 13.2 kV has an inertia constant of $H = 9$ kW-sec/kVA. Find the kinetic energy stored in the rotor at synchronous speed.

Solution : Rating of the machine

$$G = 20 \text{ MVA}$$

Given Inertia constant

$$H = 9 \text{ kW-sec/kVA}$$

$$= 9 \text{ MJ/MVA}$$

$$= \frac{\text{Stored energy in Megajoules}}{\text{Rating in MVA}} = \frac{W}{G}$$

Kinetic energy stored in rotor

$$W = GH = 9 \times 20 = 180 \text{ MJ.}$$

Example 5.4. A 100 MVA, 2 pole, 60 Hz generator has a moment of inertia 5×10^3 kg-m^2. Calculate energy stored in the rotor at rated speed. Also calculate the inertia constant H and angular momentum of the rotor at rated speed.

Solution : Synchronous speed of generator rotor

$$N = \frac{120f}{P} = \frac{120 \times 60}{2} = 3600 \text{ rpm}$$

Rated angular speed of the rotor

$$\omega = \frac{2\pi N}{60} = \frac{2\pi \times 3600}{60} \text{ rad/sec}$$

Stored energy at rated speed

$$W = \frac{1}{2} J\omega^2 = \frac{1}{2}(5 \times 10^3)\left[\frac{2\pi \times 3600}{60}\right]^2$$

$$= 355.3 \text{ MJ}$$

Rating of the machine

$$G = 100 \text{ MVA (given)}$$

Inertia constant

$$H = \frac{\text{Energy stored } W}{\text{Rated of machine } G} = \frac{355.3}{100} = 3.553 \text{ MJ/MVA}$$

Angular momentum

$$M = \frac{GH}{180f} = \frac{100 \times 3.553}{180 \times 60} = 0.0329 \text{ MJ-sec/ele. degree.}$$

Example 5.5. A 200 MVA, 50 Hz, 4 pole generator has an inertia constant of 6 MJ/MVA. Another generator 150 MVA, 3000 rpm having inertia constant 4 MJ/MVA is put in parallel with this generator. Find the inertia constant of equivalent generator on a base of 100 MVA.

Solution : Rating of first generator $G_1 = 200$ MVA

Inertia constant of first generator $H_1 = 6$ MJ/MVA

Rating of second generator $G_2 = 150$ MVA

Inertia constant of second generator $H_2 = 4$ MJ/MVA

Base MVA $G_{base} = 100$ MVA

The inertia constant of equivalent generator at 100 MVA base

$$H_{eq} = \frac{H_1 G_1}{G_{base}} + \frac{H_2 G_2}{G_{base}} = \frac{6 \times 200}{100} + \frac{4 \times 150}{100} = 18 \text{ MJ/MVA.}$$

5.6 SWING EQUATION

A generator receives mechanical torque input T_i via shaft from the prime mover and develops electromagnetic torque T_e which opposes the mechanical torque input T_i. The algebraic difference between T_i and T_e is the net accelerating torque T_a which causes acceleration of rotor.

So $$T_a = T_i - T_e \qquad ...(5.15)$$

When the machine is in steady state, the mechanical torque T_i and electromagnetic torque T_e are equal so that accelerating torque T_a is zero and there is no acceleration. When there is a sudden change in T_i or T_e there is a net accelerating torque (retarding torque if T_a is negative) on the machine. From the laws of mechanics

$$J\alpha = T_a \qquad ...(5.16)$$

where J = moment of inertia in Kg-m^2 of the machine, and

α = angular acceleration in electrical degrees/sec^2.

If θ be the angular position of rotor then

$$\alpha = \frac{d^2\theta}{dt^2} \qquad ...(5.17)$$

From Eqs. (5.16) and (5.17)

$$J\frac{d^2\theta}{dt^2} = T_a \qquad ...(5.18)$$

The angular position θ of the rotor continuously varies with time. It is convenient to measure the angular position with respect to a synchronously rotating reference axis instead of with reference to stationary axis. If we choose rotor angle δ with respect to a synchronously rotating reference frame moving with constant velocity ω then

$$\delta = \theta - \omega t$$

giving $$\frac{d^2\theta}{dt^2} = \frac{d^2\delta}{dt^2} \qquad ...(5.19)$$

From Eqs. (5.15), (5.18) and (5.19)

$$J\frac{d^2\delta}{dt^2} = T_a = T_i - T_e \qquad ...(5.20)$$

Multiplying Eq. (5.20) by rotor speed ω we get

$$J\omega \frac{d^2\delta}{dt^2} = \omega T_a = \omega T_i - \omega T_e$$

or

$$M \frac{d^2\delta}{dt^2} = P_a = P_i - P_e \quad \text{...(5.21)}$$

where, $M = J\omega$ = angular momentum

$P_i = \omega T_i$ = mechanical power input, corrected for windage and friction losses

$P_e = \omega T_e$ = electrical power output, corrected for electrical losses

$P_a = P_i - P_e$ = accelerating power or difference between input and output, each corrected for losses.

The Eq. (5.21) is known as swing equation. Each machine in a power system has its own swing equation. The electrical power P_e is the real power output of the machine. The angle δ for a machine in a large power system is same as the angle of its voltage behind transient reactance with respect to a reference bus. The swing equations, when solved for machine rotor angles δ, provide information for transient stability of the system.

For a system having only one machine connected to an infinite bus (which can provide or absorb infinite power without changing its voltage magnitude and phase angle) the angle δ is same as the angle of voltage behind transient reactance with respect to the infinite bus and is called the power angle. The angle δ swings around its steady state value during transient period and is governed by the swing equation. If angle δ, after swinging, ultimately comes to rest then the system is said to be stable, otherwise it is said to be unstable. The stability of one machine connected to an infinite bus can be determined by Equal Area Criterion.

Example 5.6. A 50 Hz, 4 pole, 100 MVA generator has an inertia constant of 8 MJ/MVA. Calculate the rotor acceleration if the mechanical input to the generator is suddenly increased to 80 MW for an electrical load of 50 MW, neglecting mechanical and electrical losses. If the acceleration is maintained for 10 cycles, calculate the change in rotor angle and rotor speed in rpm at the end of this period.

Solution : Rating of the generator $G = 100$ MVA

Inertia Constant $H = 8$ MJ/MVA

Therefore angular momentum

$$M = (GH/180f) = (100 \times 8/180 \times 50)$$

$$= 0.08889 \text{ MJ-sec/elect. degree}$$

Mechanical power input

$$P_i = 80 \text{ MW}$$

Electrical power output

$$P_e = 50 \text{ MW}$$

Accelerating power

$$P_a = P_i - P_e = 80 - 50 = 30 \text{ MW}$$

From swing equation

$$M \frac{d^2\delta}{dt^2} = P_a$$

therefore $0.08889 \times \dfrac{d^2\delta}{dt^2} = 30$

Hence acceleration

$$\frac{d^2\delta}{dt^2} = \frac{30}{0.08889} = 337.5 \text{ elect. degree/sec}^2 = \alpha$$

The acceleration α is maintained for 10 cycles which are completed in time

$$t = (10/f) \text{ sec.}$$

$$= (10/50) = 0.2 \text{ sec.}$$

Therefore in 10 cycles (or 0.2 sec.)

$$\text{change in } \delta = \frac{1}{2}\alpha t^2 = \frac{1}{2}(337.5) \times (0.2)^2 = 6.75 \text{ elect. degree}$$

Due to the acceleration the rotor speed increases from synchronous speed to above synchronous in 10 cycles. The synchronous speed of the rotor is

$$N = \frac{120 \times 50}{4} = 1500 \text{ rpm}$$

$= (360 \times 1500)/60$ elect. degree/sec = 9000 elect. degree/sec.

Rotor speed at the end of 10 cycles (0.2 sec.)

$= 9000 + \alpha t = 9000 + (337.5 \times 0.2) = 9067.5$ elect. degree/sec

$= (9067.5 \times 60/360)$ rpm = 1511.25 rpm.

5.7 EQUAL AREA CRITERION

The stability of single machine swinging with respect to an infinite bus can be determined by the use of equal area criterion. Fig. 5.12 shows a machine connected to an infinite bus through a reactance X.

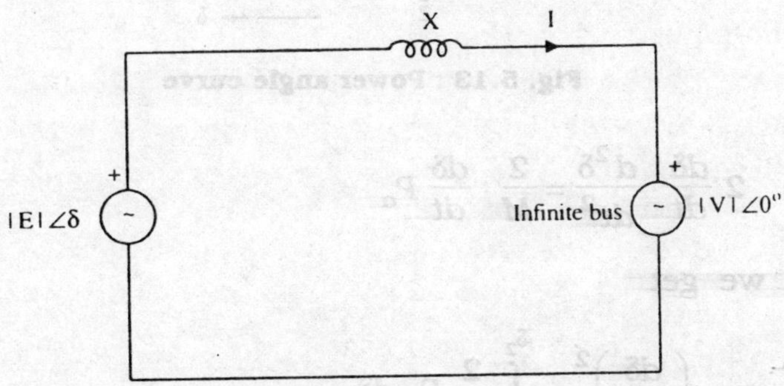

Fig. 5.12 : One machine connected to an infinite bus

The real power transmitted to infinite bus

$$P_e = \frac{|E|\ |V|}{X} \sin \delta$$

or $$P_e = P_m \sin \delta \qquad \text{...(5.22)}$$

where $P_m = \dfrac{|E|\ |V|}{X}$ which is also equal to the steady state stability limit of the system. Fig. 5.13 shows the power angle curve for the machine.

The swing equation of the machine is given by

$$M \frac{d^2\delta}{dt^2} = P_a \qquad \text{...(5.23)}$$

where $$P_a = P_i - P_e \qquad \text{...(5.24)}$$

Multiplying both the sides of Eq. 5.23 by $\dfrac{2}{M} \cdot \dfrac{d\delta}{dt}$ we get

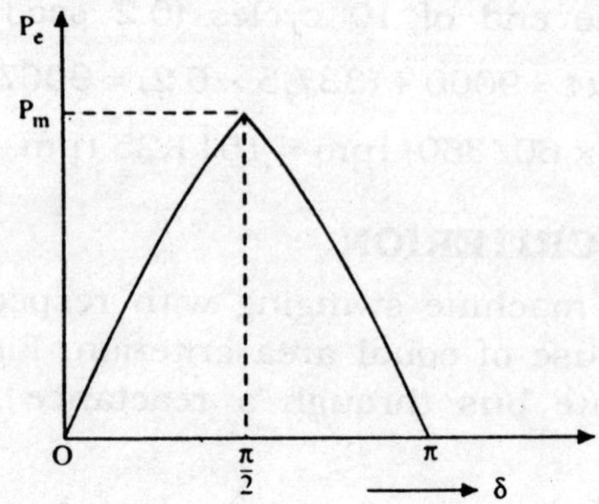

Fig. 5.13 : Power angle curve

$$2\frac{d\delta}{dt}\cdot\frac{d^2\delta}{dt^2}=\frac{2}{M}\cdot\frac{d\delta}{dt}P_a$$

Integrating we get

$$\left(\frac{d\delta}{dt}\right)^2=\int_{\delta_1}^{\delta_2}\frac{2}{M}P_a\,d\delta \qquad ...(5.25)$$

where δ_1 and δ_2 are the lower and upper limits of power angle δ upto which the rotor swings during transient period. From Eq. (5.25)

$$\frac{d\delta}{dt}=\sqrt{\int_{\delta_1}^{\delta_2}\frac{2}{M}P_a\,d\delta}$$

For stable operation $\frac{d\delta}{dt}=0$ after the transient period is over.

Hence $\int_{\delta_1}^{\delta_2}P_a\,d\delta=0$ for stable operation.

Using Eq. (5.24) we get

$$\int_{\delta_1}^{\delta_2}(P_i-P_e)\,d\delta=0$$

Using Eq. (5.22) it becomes

$$\int_{\delta_1}^{\delta_2} (P_i - P_m \sin\delta)\, d\delta = 0 \qquad \text{...(5.26)}$$

The integral given by Eq. (5.26) may be interpreted graphically as shown in Fig. 5.14 assuming that P_i remains constant.

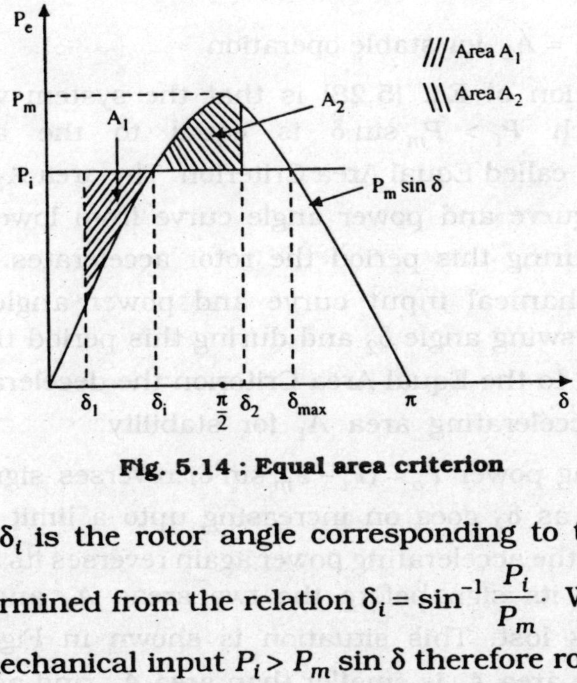

Fig. 5.14 : Equal area criterion

In Fig. 5.14, δ_i is the rotor angle corresponding to the mechanical input P_i and can be determined from the relation $\delta_i = \sin^{-1}\dfrac{P_i}{P_m}$. When the rotor swings from δ_1 to δ_i the mechanical input $P_i > P_m \sin\delta$ therefore rotor accelerates. When rotor swings from δ_i to δ_2 the mechanical input $P_i < P_m \sin\delta$ therefore the rotor retards.

The Eq. (5.26) represents condition for stable operation which can be written as

$$\int_{\delta_1}^{\delta_i} (P_i - P_m \sin\delta)\, d\delta + \int_{\delta_i}^{\delta_2} (P_i - P_m \sin\delta)\, d\delta = 0$$

or

$$\int_{\delta_1}^{\delta_i} (P_i - P_m \sin\delta)\, d\delta - \int_{\delta_i}^{\delta_2} (P_m \sin\delta - P_i)\, d\delta = 0$$

or
$$\int_{\delta_1}^{\delta_i} (P_i - P_m \sin \delta)\, d\delta = \int_{\delta_i}^{\delta_2} (P_m \sin \delta - P_i)\, d\delta \qquad \text{...(5.27)}$$

The term $\int_{\delta_1}^{\delta_i} (P_i - P_m \sin \delta)\, d\delta$ represents area A_1 in Fig. 5.14 and the term $\int_{\delta_i}^{\delta_2} (P_m \sin \delta - P_i)\, d\delta$ represents area A_2. Substituting in Eq. (5.27) gives

$$A_1 = A_2 \text{ for stable operation} \qquad \text{...(5.28)}$$

The interpretation of Eq. (5.28) is that the system will be stable if the area A_1 for which $P_i > P_m \sin \delta$ is equal to the area A_2 for which $P_i < P_m \sin \delta$. This is called Equal Area Criterion. The area A_1 is the area between mechanical input curve and power angle curve from lower swing angle δ_1 to the angle δ_i and during this period the rotor accelerates. The area A_2 is the area between mechanical input curve and power angle curve from angle δ_i to the maximum swing angle δ_2 and during this period the rotor decelerates. Therefore according to the Equal Area Criterion the decelerating area A_2 should be equal to the accelerating area A_1 for stability.

The accelerating power $P_a = (P_i - P_m \sin \delta)$ reverses sign at δ_i. The area A_2 goes on increasing as δ_2 goes on increasing upto a limit δ_{max}, shown in Fig. 5.14, beyond which the accelerating power again reverses its sign. If the accelerating power reverses its sign before the two areas A_1 and A_2 become equal, the synchronism is lost. This situation is shown in Fig. 5.15.

In Fig. 5.15 the area A_2 is smaller than area A_1, and as δ increases beyond δ_{max} (at which $P_a = 0$) the accelerating power changes its sign so that the area A_2 can no longer increase. Instead the area A_2 is now to be compared with $A_1 + A_3$. Clearly the area for $P_i < P_m \sin \delta$ can not become equal to the area for $P_i > P_m \sin \delta$, if $\delta_2 > \delta_{max}$ and so the system is unstable. Thus the limit of stability occurs when the angle δ_2 is such that at this point $P_a = 0$ *i.e.*, $P_i = P_m \sin \delta$ and the areas A_1 and A_2 are equal. For this case δ_2 coincides with the angle δ_{max} on the power angle curve at $P_i = P_m \sin \delta$ and $\delta > (\pi/2)$. From the geometry of Fig. 5.15, the limiting value of δ_2 for stability is $\delta_{max} = (\pi - \delta_i)$.

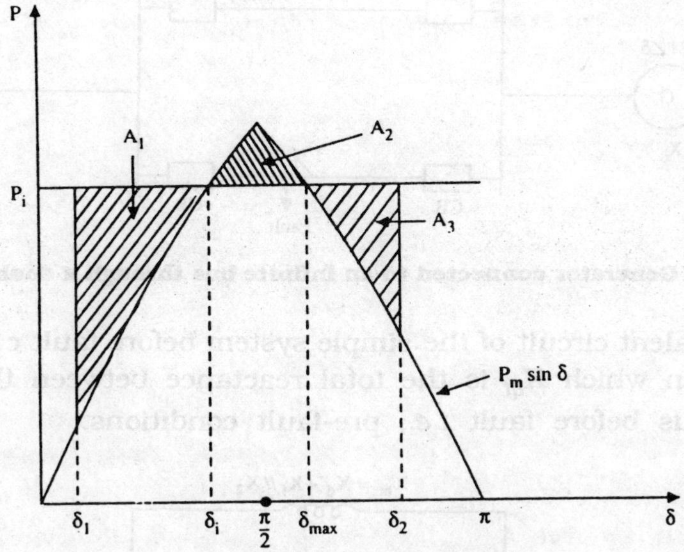

Fig. 5.15 : Equal area criterion for an unstable system

The stability of a system using Equal Area Criterion is generally determined as follows. Given the value of mechanical power input P_i the value of δ_i is determined using relation $P_i = P_m \sin \delta_i$. The value of δ_1 can be determined from the given data for this purpose. The area A_1 from angle δ_1 to δ_i is calculated first. Then the maximum possible area $A_{2,\,max}$ from angle δ_i to $(\pi - \delta_i)$ is calculated next. If $A_{2,\,max} \geq A_1$ the system is stable and if $A_{2,\,max} < A_1$ then the system is unstable.

5.8 APPLICATIONS OF EQUAL AREA CRITERION

The use of the equal area criterion is illustrated by applying it to three simple cases :

1. A sustained line fault
2. A line fault cleared after the lapse of a certain time by the simultaneous opening of the circuit breakers at both ends of the line.
3. Case (2) followed by reclosing.

The fault is assumed to occur at point F of the simple system shown in Fig. 5.16 which consists of a generator connected through a double circuit line to an infinite bus.

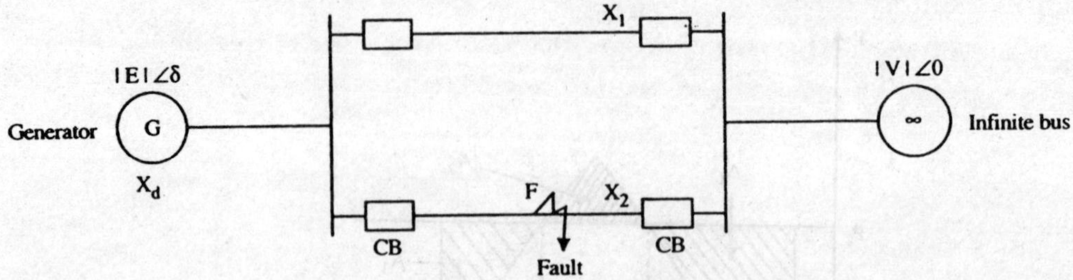

Fig. 5.16 : Generator connected to an infinite bus through a double circuit line

The equivalent circuit of the simple system before fault can be represented by Fig. 5.17 in which X_{bf} is the total reactance between the generator and the infinite bus before fault *i.e.*, pre-fault conditions.

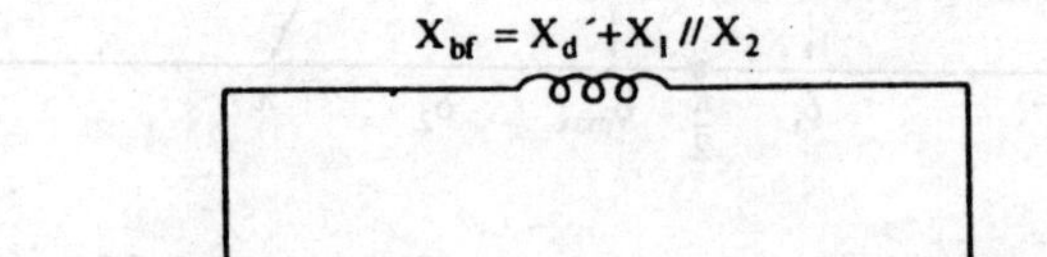

Fig. 5.17 : Equivalent circuit before fault (pre-fault conditions)

The equivalent circuit of the system during fault is developed in Figs. 5.18 (*a*) to 5.18 (*b*). The star connected reactances in Fig. 5.18 (*a*) are converted

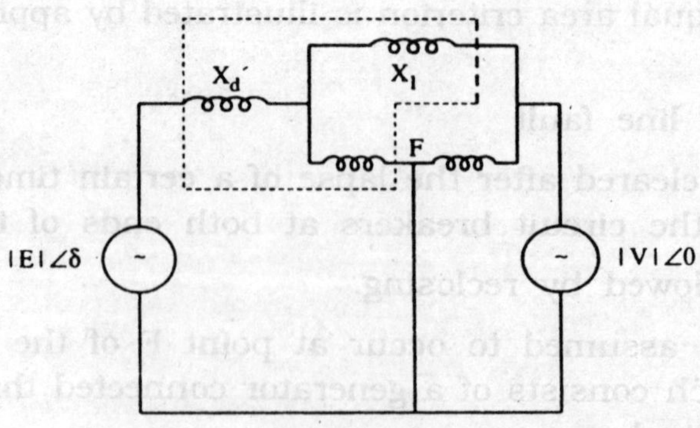

Fig. 5.18 (*a*)

into equivalent delta in Fig. 5.18 (*b*) in which the reactance X_{df} is the net reactance between the generator and the infinite bus during fault.

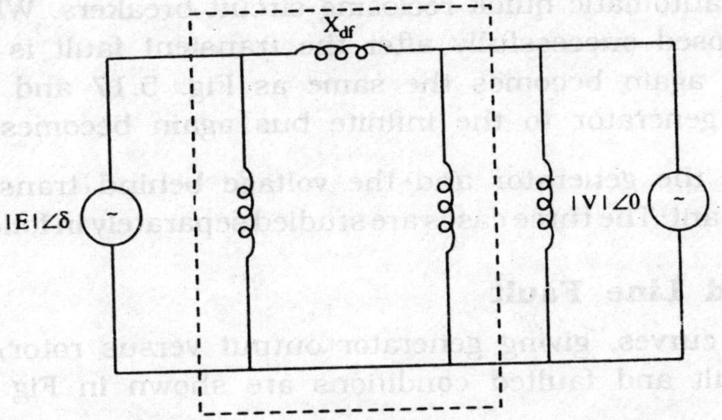

Fig. 5.18 (*b*) : Equivalent circuit during fault

The equivalent circuit of the system after the fault is cleared by opening circuit breakers at the both ends of the faulted line, can be represented by Fig. 5.19 in which X_{pf} is the total reactance between the generator and the infinite bus after fault is cleared *i.e.*, post-fault conditions.

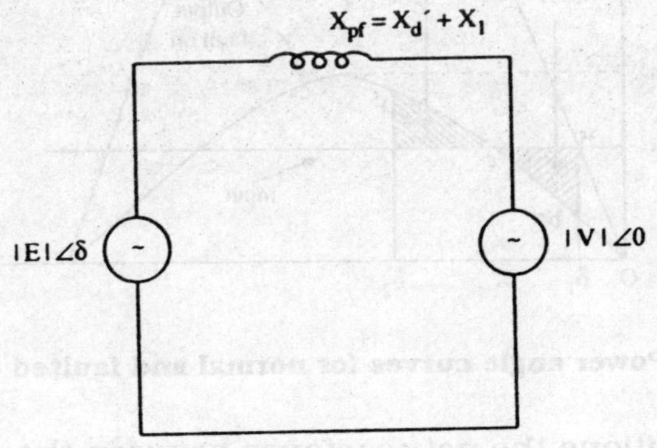

Fig. 5.19 : Equivalent circuit after fault is cleared (post-fault)

A little consideration will conclude that $X_{bf} < X_{pf} < X_{df}$, if generator reactances are very small as compared with the total reactance of transmission line, which is usually the case. If p_{m1}, P_{m2} and P_{m3} are the maximum power flows from generator to infinite bus in pre-fault (before fault), during fault and post-fault conditions then $P_{m1} > P_{m3} > P_{m2}$ as maximum power flow is inversely proportional to the reactance.

Most of the faults are of transient nature. The transmission lines may be provided with automatic quick reclosing circuit breakers. When the circuit breakers are reclosed successfully after the transient fault is over then the equivalent circuit again becomes the same as Fig. 5.17 and the maximum power flow from generator to the infinite bus again becomes P_{m1}.

The input to the generator and the voltage behind transient reactance are assumed constant. The three cases are studied separately in following sections.

5.8.1 Sustained Line Fault

The power angle curves, giving generator output versus rotor/voltage angle, for normal/prefault and faulted conditions are shown in Fig. 5.20.

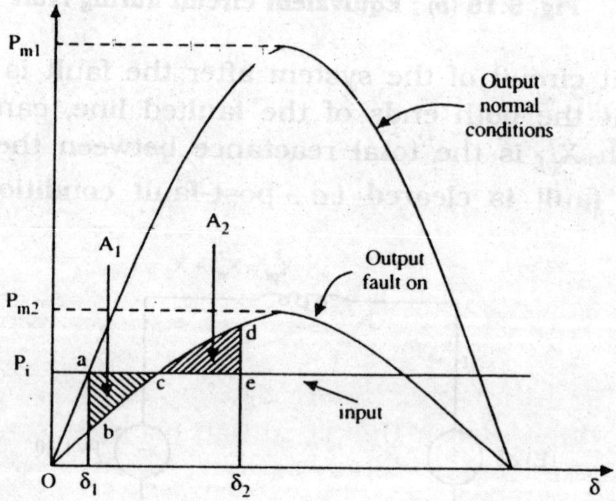

Fig. 5.20 : Power angle curves for normal and faulted conditions

During fault conditions the net reactance between the generator and infinite bus increases and generator terminal voltage reduces. Therefore the maximum power flow between generator and infinite bus during the fault reduces to P_{m2} as compared with that of normal conditions in which it is P_{m1}. The horizontal line at distance P_i above the axis represents the constant input. The initial operating point is a at the intersection of the input and normal output curves. The initial rotor angle is δ_1 and its speed is synchronous speed. When the fault occurs the operating point drops to b, directly below a, on the fault output curve. The rotor angle remains δ_1 at the instant of fault occurrence. There is then an accelerating power, $P_a = (P_i - P_{m2} \sin \delta_1)$, represented by the length ab. As a consequence the generator is accelerated, rotor angle increases, and the operating point moves along the curve from b toward c. As it does so, the accelerating power and the acceleration decrease, becoming zero at c. At this point, however, the speed of the generator is greater than that of the synchronous speed, represented by rotor speed of infinite bus, and the angle δ continues to increase. As it does so, accelerating power P_a becomes negative, representing retarding power. The speed reduces until at point d, determined by the equality of area $A_1 = abc$ and area $A_2 = cde$, it becomes equal to the synchronous speed. There is still a retarding power, therefore, the speed of the generator continues to decrease, becoming less than that of the infinite bus. The rotor angle δ decreases, and the operating point moves from d toward b through c. The system is stable. The operating point would continue to oscillate between b and d if there is no damping. Actually oscillations diminish due to damping present, and the operating point finally rests at point c.

If the initial load on the generator is increased, as represented by raising the input line P_i, the areas A_1 and A_2 and the maximum swing δ_2 increase. The greatest value which P_i can have without the machine going out of step during the existence of fault is that value which makes δ_2 occur at intersection of the input curve and the fault output curve, as shown in Fig. 5.21. Here the critical condition is reached in which both, the speed deviation from synchronous speed and the acceleration, become zero simultaneously at angle δ_2. The value of P_i which makes this condition occur is the transient stability limit.

If the initial load is still larger, then area A_2 in Fig. 5.21 is smaller than area A_1. The generator reaches at operating point e on the curve, where the acceleration is zero, with the speed more than synchronous. Consequently δ continues to increase and, as it does so, the accelerating power becomes positive. The system is unstable. In this case there is some retardation (between points c and e), but not enough to prevent loss of synchronism.

If the input P_i is greater than P_{m2}, the maximum output with the fault there is no retardation at all and the system is unstable with the sustained fault.

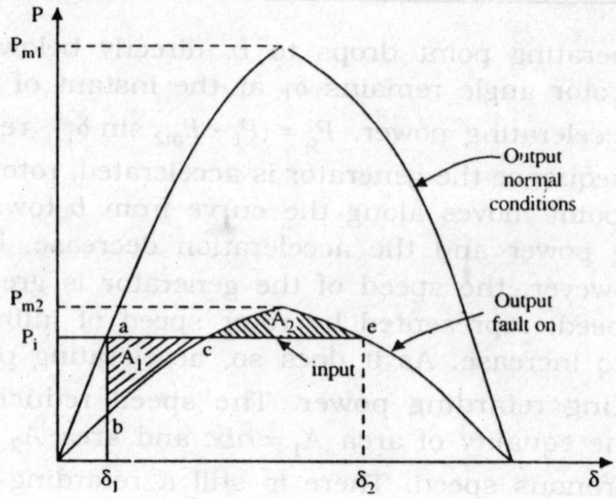

Fig. 5.21 : The input line raised from Fig. 5.20 until δ_2 reaches to point *e*.

5.8.2 Line Fault with Subsequent Clearing

In this case three power-angle curves are needed :

1. for the normal or prefault condition with the system intact,
2. for the fault condition, and
3. for the post-fault or cleared condition with the faulted line disconnected.

These curves are shown in Fig. 5.22.

As in the case of sustained fault, the initial angle δ_1 is determined by the intersection of the input line and the prefault output curve (point *a*). Occurrence of the fault causes the operating point to drop from *a* to *b* on the fault output curve, and the accelerating power causes it to move along the curve from point *b* to *c*. We may assume that, when point *c* is reached, the circuit breakers open, clearing the fault. The operating point then jumps up to *e* on the post-fault output curve and travels along that curve to *f*, where area $A_2 = defg$ equals area $A_1 = abcd$.

If initial output of generator is higher than that shown in Fig. 5.22, the post-fault operating point *f* moves to the right until at the stability limit the point *f* coincides with point *h*. A still higher initial output leads to instability.

Another factor which causes point *f* to move to the right is an increase in the time of clearing the fault, resulting in a larger clearing angle δ_c. For any given initial load there is a critical clearing angle. If the actual clearing

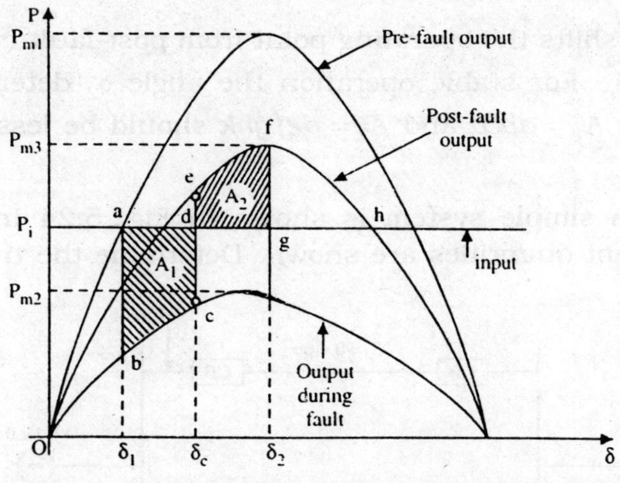

Fig. 5.22 : Power angle curves with fault cleared at δ_c

angle is smaller than the critical value, the system is stable; if larger, the system is unstable.

5.8.3 Line Fault with Subsequent Clearing followed by Reclosing

Fig. 5.23 shows the application of equal area criterion for such a case. The

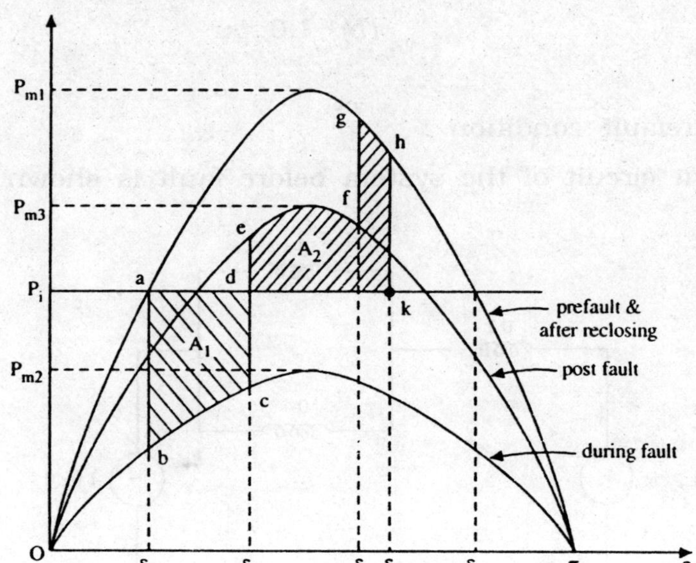

Fig. 5.23 : Power angle curves with reclosing at δ_r

reclosing at angle δ_r, shifts the operating point from post-fault curve to pre-fault curve at the angle δ_r. For stable operation the angle δ_2 determined from the equality of the areas $A_1 = abcd$ and $A_2 = defghk$ should be less then δ_m shown in Fig. 5.23.

Example 5.7. A simple system is shown in Fig. 5.24 in which the per unit values of different quantities are shown. Determine the transient stability

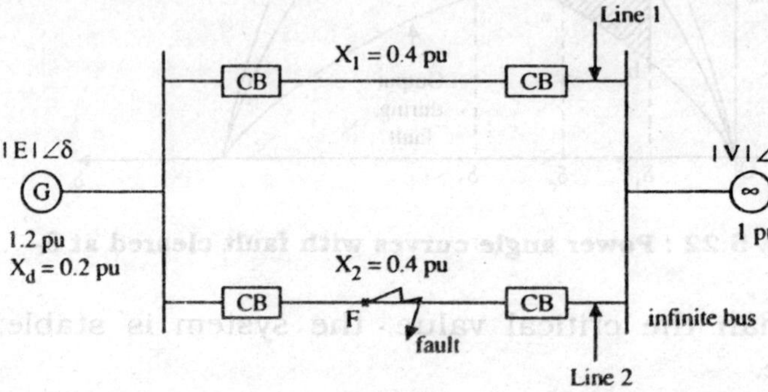

Fig. 5.24

of the system and maximum rotor swing for a balanced 3-phase sustained fault occurring at mid-point of line-2 when the power transfer is

(*a*) 0.8 pu (*b*) 1.0 pu

(*c*) 1.5 pu.

Solution : Prefault condition :

The equivalent circuit of the system before fault is shown in Fig. 5.25.

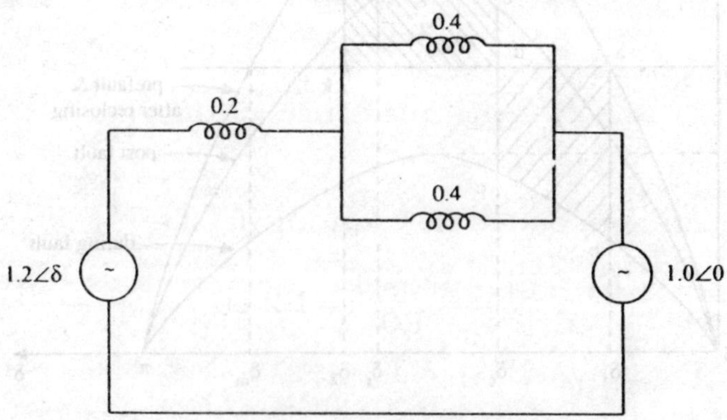

Fig. 5.25 : Equivalent circuit before fault

From Fig. 5.25 the transfer reactance before fault

$$X = 0.2 + \frac{0.4 \times 0.4}{0.4 + 0.4} = 0.4 \text{ pu}$$

Therefore maximum power flow before fault

$$P_{m1} = \frac{|E| \ |V|}{X} = \frac{1.2 \times 1}{0.4} = 3 \text{ pu}$$

and power flow before fault

$$P_{e1} = P_{m1} \sin \delta = 3 \sin \delta$$

During fault condition :

For the fault at mid-point of line-2 the equivalent circuit is developed in Figs. 5.26 and 5.27. The star network of Fig. 5.26 is converted into equivalent delta in Fig. 5.27.

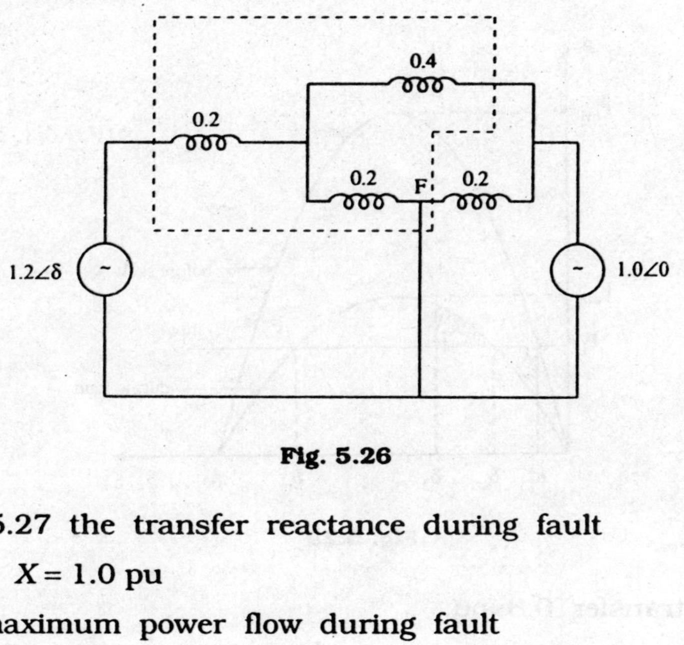

Fig. 5.26

From Fig. 5.27 the transfer reactance during fault

$$X = 1.0 \text{ pu}$$

Therefore maximum power flow during fault

$$P_{m2} = \frac{|E| \ |V|}{X} = \frac{1.2 \times 1}{1.0} = 1.2 \text{ pu}$$

and power flow during fault

$$P_{e2} = P_{m2} \sin \delta = 1.2 \sin \delta$$

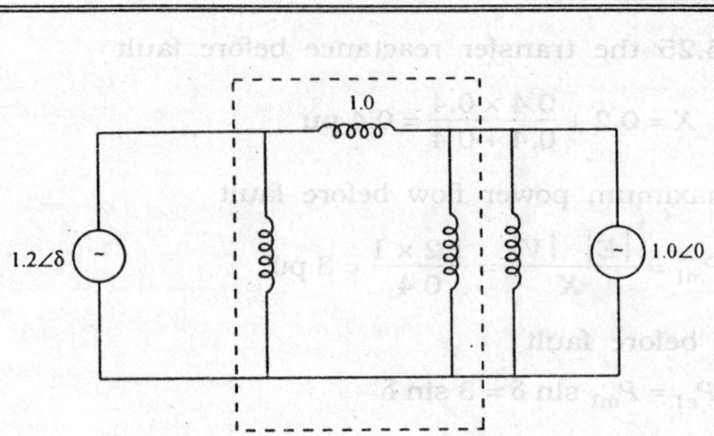

Fig. 5.27

The power angle curves before fault and during fault are shown in Fig. 5.28.

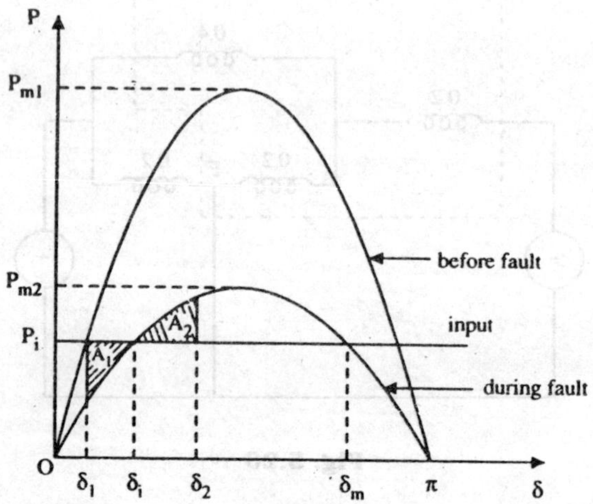

Fig. 5.28

(*a*) With power transfer 0.8 pu.

As the system is in equilibrium before fault therefore the mechanical input P_i before fault is equal to the power transfer before fault. Therefore

$$P_i = 0.8 \text{ pu.}$$

The mechanical input is considered constant during the transient period. The power angle before fault is given by the equation

$$P_i = P_{m1} \sin \delta_1$$

or $$0.8 = 3 \sin \delta_1$$

or $$\delta_1 = \sin^{-1} (0.8/3) = 0.27 \text{ rad.} = 15.5^o$$

When the fault occurs the rotor angle can not change instantaneously but the operating point drops to the fault output curve. The generator accelerates during the fault from angle δ_1 to angle δ_i as shown in Fig. 5.28 because the output is less than the input during this period. The angle δ_i is given by the equation

$$P_i = P_{m2} \sin \delta_i$$

or $$0.8 = 1.2 \sin \delta_i$$

or $$\delta_i = \sin^{-1} (0.8/1.2) = 0.73 \text{ rad.} = 41.8^o.$$

The accelerating area

$$A_1 = \int_{\delta_1}^{\delta_i} (P_i - P_{m2} \sin \delta)\ d\delta = \int_{0.27}^{0.73} (0.8 - 1.2 \sin \delta)\ d\delta$$

$$A_1 = [0.8\delta + 1.2 \cos \delta]_{0.27}^{0.73}$$

$$= 0.8\ (0.73 - 0.27) + 1.2\ (\cos 0.73 - \cos 0.27)$$

$$= 0.368 + (-0.262)$$

$$= 0.1057$$

For stability the rotor may swing from δ_i upto the maximum angle δ_m where $\delta_m = \pi - \delta_i = \pi - 0.73 = 2.41$ rad $= 138.1^o$. The maximum retarding area $A_{2,\,max}$ is given by

$$A_{2,\,max} = \int_{\delta_i}^{\delta_m} (P_{m2} \sin \delta - P_i)\ d\delta = \int_{0.73}^{2.41} (1.2 \sin \delta - 0.8)\ d\delta$$

$$A_{2,\,max} = [-1.2 \cos \delta - 0.8\delta]_{0.73}^{2.41}$$

$$= -1.2\ (\cos 2.41 - \cos 0.73) - 0.8\ (2.41 - 0.73)$$

$$= 1.7871 - 1.344$$

$$= 0.4431$$

Since $A_{2,\max} > A_1$ therefore the system is stable. The maximum value of rotor swing δ_2 is given by the condition

$$A_2 = A_1$$

or $$\int_{\delta_i}^{\delta_2} (P_{m2} \sin \delta - P_i)\, d\delta = 0.1057$$

or $$\int_{0.73}^{\delta_2} (1.2 \sin \delta - 0.8)\, d\delta = 0.1057$$

or $$[-1.2 \cos \delta - 0.8\delta]_{0.73}^{\delta_2} = 0.1057$$

or $$-1.2 (\cos \delta_2 - \cos 0.73) - 0.8 (\delta_2 - 0.73) = 0.1057$$

or $$-1.2 \cos \delta_2 + 0.894 - 0.8\delta_2 + 0.584 = 0.1057$$

or $$1.3723 = 1.2 \cos \delta_2 + 0.8\delta_2$$

Using iterative method for solution gives $\delta_2 = 1.267$ rad $= 72.6°$.

(*b*) With power transfer 1.0 pu.

As the system is in equilibrium before fault therefore the mechanical input P_i before fault is equal to the power transfer before fault. Therefore

$$P_i = 1.0 \text{ pu.}$$

The mechanical input is considered constant during the transient period. The power angle before fault is given by the equation

$$P_i = P_{m1} \sin \delta_1$$

or $$1.0 = 3 \sin \delta_1$$

or $$\delta_1 = \sin^{-1} (1.0/3) = 0.34 \text{ rad.} = 19.5°$$

When the fault occurs the rotor angle can not change instantaneously but the operating point drops to the fault output curve. The generator accelerates during the fault from angle δ_1 to angle δ_i as shown in Fig. 5.28 because the output is less than the input during this period. The angle δ_i is given by the equation

$$P_i = P_{m2} \sin \delta_i$$

or $$1.0 = 1.2 \sin \delta_i$$

or $$\delta_i = \sin^{-1} (1.0/1.2) = 0.985 \text{ rad.} = 56.4^\circ.$$

The accelerating area

$$A_1 = \int_{\delta_i}^{\delta_i} (P_i - P_{m2} \sin \delta)\, d\delta = \int_{0.34}^{0.985} (1.0 - 1.2 \sin \delta)\, d\delta$$

$$A_1 = [\delta + 1.2 \cos \delta]_{0.34}^{0.985}$$

$$= (0.985 - 0.34) + 1.2 (\cos 0.985 - \cos 0.34)$$

$$= 0.645 + (-0.468)$$

$$= 0.177$$

For stability the rotor may swing from δ_i upto the maximum angle δ_m where $\delta_m = \pi - \delta_i = \pi - 0.985 = 2.157$ rad. = 123.6°. The maximum retarding area $A_{2,\,max}$ is given by

$$A_{2,\,max} = \int_{\delta_i}^{\delta_m} (P_{m2} \sin \delta - P_i)\, d\delta = \int_{0.985}^{2.157} (1.2 \sin \delta - 1.0)\, d\delta$$

$$A_{2,\,max} = [-1.2 \cos \delta - \delta]_{0.985}^{2.157}$$

$$= -1.2 (\cos 2.157 - \cos 0.985) - (2.157 - 0.985)$$

$$= 1.327 - 1.172$$

$$= 0.155$$

Since $A_{2,\,max} < A_1$ therefore the system is unstable. The maximum rotor swing is unbounded.

(c) With power transfer 1.5 pu.

The maximum possible value of power transfer during fault condition is $P_{m2} = 1.2$ pu. Since the initial load is 1.5 pu therefore stability is impossible for a sustained fault. The maximum rotor swing is unbounded.

Example 5.8. A balanced 3-phase fault occurs at mid-point of line-2 when the power transfer is 1.5 pu in the system shown in Fig. 5.24.

(*a*) Is the system stable when the fault is cleared at power angle $\delta = 60^\circ$? If so find the maximum rotor swing.

(*b*) Find the critical clearing angle.

(*c*) Find the critical clearing angle if a 3-phase fault occurs on the line-2 close to the generator bus.

Solution : In this case the power-angle curves needed are for the before fault (prefault), during fault and postfault (after the fault is cleared) conditions. The power-angle curves for prefault and during fault conditions have already been computed in Example 5.7. The power-angle curve for the post fault condition is computed below.

The equivalent circuit of the system under post fault conditions is shown in Fig. 5.29.

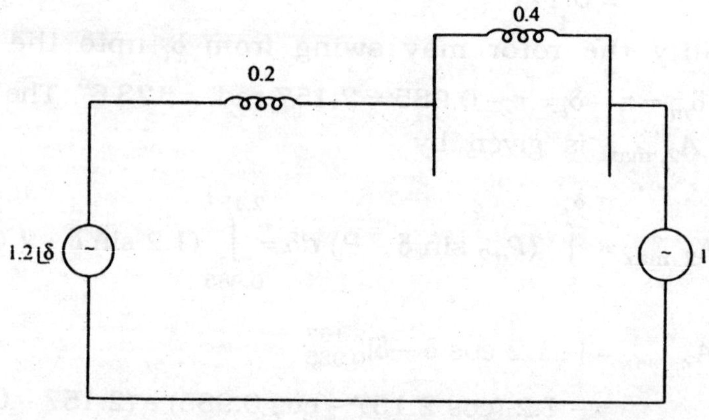

Fig. 5.29

From Fig. 5.29, the transfer reactance under post fault conditions

$$X = 0.2 + 0.4 = 0.6 \text{ pu}$$

Therefore maximum power flow under post fault conditions

$$P_{m3} = \frac{|E|\ |V|}{X} = \frac{1.2 \times 1}{0.6} = 2.0 \text{ pu}$$

and power flow under post fault conditions

$$P_{e3} = P_{m3} \sin \delta = 2 \sin \delta$$

The three power angle curves are shown in Fig. 5.30.

As the system is in equilibrium before fault therefore the mechanical input P_i before fault is equal to the power transfer before fault. Therefore

$$P_i = 1.5 \text{ pu.}$$

The mechanical input is considered constant during the transient period. The power angle before fault is given by the equation

$$P_i = P_{m1} \sin \delta_1$$

or $$1.5 = 3 \sin \delta_1$$

or $$\delta_1 = \sin^{-1} (1.5/3) = 0.524 \text{ rad.} = 30^\circ$$

When the fault occurs the rotor angle can not change instantaneously but the operating point drops to the fault output curve. The generator accelerates during the fault from angle δ_1 to clearing angle δ_c as shown in Fig. 5.30 because the output is less than the input during this period. Given that the clearing angle

$$\delta_c = 60^\circ = 1.047 \text{ rad.}$$

The accelerating area

$$A_1 = \int_{\delta_1}^{\delta_c} (P_i - P_{m2} \sin \delta)\, d\delta = \int_{0.524}^{1.047} (1.5 - 1.2 \sin \delta)\, d\delta$$

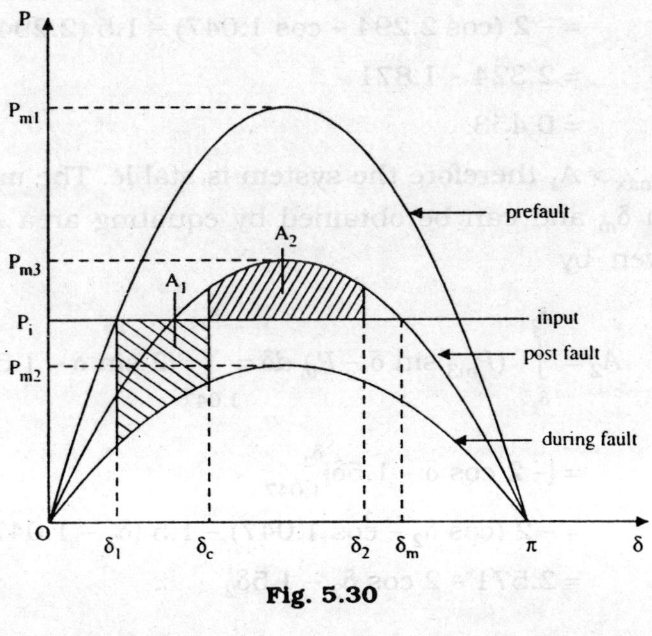

Fig. 5.30

$$= [1.5\delta + 1.2\cos\delta]_{0.524}^{1.047}$$

$$= (1.571 - 0.786) + 1.2\,(\cos 1.057 - \cos 0.524)$$

$$= 0.785 + (-0.439)$$

$$= 0.346$$

For stability the rotor may swing from δ_c upto the maximum angle δ_m where $\delta_m = \pi - \delta_i$. The angle δ_i is given by the equation

$$P_i = P_{m3} \sin \delta_i$$

or $$1.5 = 2 \sin \delta_i$$

or $$\delta_i = \sin^{-1}(1.5/2) = 0.848 \text{ rad.}$$

Therefore $\delta_m = \pi - \delta_i = \pi - 0.848 = 2.294$ rad. $= 131.4^\circ$

The rotor decelerates from δ_c to maximum possible swing angle δ_m. The maximum available decelerating area $A_{2,\,max}$ is given by

$$A_{2,\,max} = \int_{\delta_c}^{\delta_m} (P_{m3} \sin \delta - P_i)\, d\delta = \int_{1.047}^{2.294} (2 \sin \delta - 1.5)\, d\delta$$

$$= [-2\cos\delta - 1.5\delta]_{1.047}^{2.294}$$

$$= -2\,(\cos 2.294 - \cos 1.047) - 1.5\,(2.294 - 1.047)$$

$$= 2.324 - 1.871$$

$$= 0.453$$

Since $A_{2,\,max} > A_1$ therefore the system is stable. The maximum rotor swing δ_2 is less than δ_m and can be obtained by equating area A_1 to area A_2 where area A_2 is given by

$$A_2 = \int_{\delta_c}^{\delta_2} (P_{m3} \sin \delta - P_i)\, d\delta = \int_{1.047}^{\delta_2} (2 \sin \delta - 1.5)\, d\delta$$

$$= [-2\cos\delta - 1.5\delta]_{1.047}^{\delta_2}$$

$$= -2\,(\cos \delta_2 - \cos 1.047) - 1.5\,(\delta_2 - 1.047)$$

$$= 2.571 - 2\cos\delta_2 - 1.5\delta_2$$

Equating the areas A_1 and A_2 gives

$$0.346 = 2.571 - 2\cos\delta_2 - 1.5\delta_2$$

or $$2\cos\delta_2 + 1.5\delta_2 = 2.225$$

The equation is non-linear in terms of δ_2 therefore can be solved by iterative method. By iterative solution one may get maximum rotor swing

$$\delta_2 = 1.847 \text{ rad.} = 105.8^\circ.$$

(*b*) **Critical clearing angle :** If the fault is cleared at critical clearing angle δ_{cc} instead of at $\delta_c = 60^\circ$ then the accelerating area A_1 from angle δ_1 to δ_{cc} is equal to the maximum available decelerating area $A_{2,\,max}$ from angle δ_{cc} to δ_m. Therefore

$$\int_{\delta_1}^{\delta_{cc}} (P_i - P_{m2}\sin\delta)\,d\delta = \int_{\delta_{cc}}^{\delta_m} (P_{m3}\sin\delta - P_i)\,d\delta$$

giving $$\int_{0.524}^{\delta_{cc}} (1.5 - 1.2\sin\delta)\,d\delta = \int_{\delta_{cc}}^{2.294} (2\sin\delta - 1.5)\,d\delta$$

or $$[1.5\delta + 1.2\cos\delta]_{0.524}^{\delta_{cc}} = [-2\cos\delta - 1.5\delta]_{\delta_{cc}}^{2.294}$$

or $$1.5\delta_{cc} - 0.786 + 1.2\cos\delta_{cc} - 1.039 = (1.324 + 2\cos\delta_{cc} - 3.441 + 1.5\,\delta_{cc})$$

or $$-0.786 - 1.039 - 1.324 + 3.441 = \cos\delta_{cc}\,(2 - 1.2)$$

or $$\cos\delta_{cc} = 0.292/0.8 = 0.365$$

or $$\delta_{cc} = 1.197 \text{ rad.} = 68.6^\circ.$$

(*c*) **Critical Clearing angle for fault close to generator bus :**

When the fault is close to the generator bus and on line-2 then during the fault no power transfer can take place because the generator bus voltage becomes zero during the fault. Therefore $P_{m2} = 0$ during fault conditions.

Now proceeding similar to case (*b*) the solution is as follows. If the fault is cleared at critical clearing angle δ_{cc} then the accelerating area A_1 from angle δ_1 to δ_{cc} is equal to the maximum available decelerating area $A_{2,\,max}$ from angle δ_{cc} to δ_m, with $P_{m2} = 0$. Therefore

$$\int_{\delta_1}^{\delta_{cc}} (P_i - 0)\, d\delta = \int_{\delta_{cc}}^{\delta_m} (P_{m3} \sin \delta - P_i)\, d\delta$$

giving $$\int_{0.524}^{\delta_{cc}} 1.5\, d\delta = \int_{\delta_{cc}}^{2.294} (2 \sin \delta - 1.5)\, d\delta$$

or $$[1.5\delta]_{0.524}^{\delta_{cc}} = [-2 \cos \delta - 1.5\delta]_{\delta_{cc}}^{2.294}$$

or $$1.5\delta_{cc} - 0.786 = 1.324 + 2 \cos \delta_{cc} - 3.441 + 1.5\delta_{cc}$$

or $$-0.786 - 1.324 + 3.441 = 2 \cos \delta_{cc}$$

or $$\cos \delta_{cc} = 1.331/2 = 0.6655$$

or $$\delta_{cc} = 0.843 \text{ rad.} = 48.28^{\circ}.$$

Example 5.9. The system shown in Fig. 5.24 is operating in equilibrium with power transfer 1.5 p.u. when one of the lines is suddenly switched out. Predict whether the system will be stable or not. If the system is stable find the maximum value which power angle δ attains.

Solution : In this case the power-angle curves needed are for the two parallel lines intact case and the line-2 switched out case. The power-angle curve for the case when both lines are intact have already been computed in Example 5.7. In this condition electrical power output is given by

$$P_{e1} = P_{m1} \sin \delta = 3 \sin \delta$$

The power-angle curve for the case when one line switched out have been computed in Example 5.8. In this condition electrical power output is given by

$$P_{e3} = P_{m3} \sin \delta = 2 \sin \delta^{\circ}$$

The two power angle curves are shown in Fig. 5.31.

As the system is in equilibrium before the line-2 is switched out therefore the mechanical input P_i is equal to the power transfer. Therefore

$$P_i = 1.5 \text{ pu.}$$

The mechanical input is considered constant during the transient period. The power angle before line-2 is switched out is given by the equation

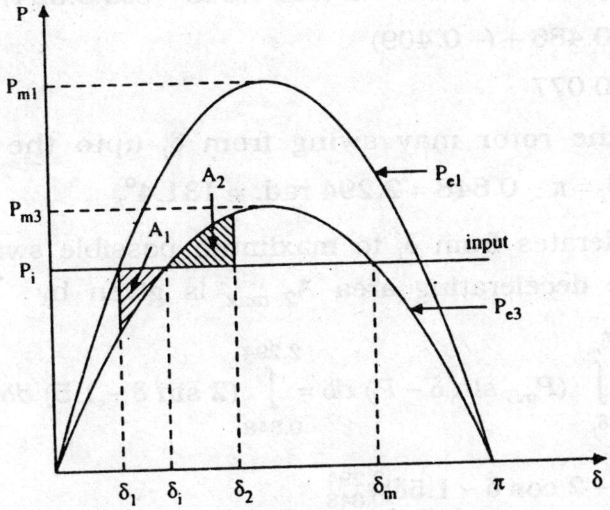

Fig. 5.31

$$P_i = P_{m1} \sin \delta_1$$

or $$1.5 = 3 \sin \delta_1$$

or $$\delta_1 = \sin^{-1} (1.5/3) = 0.524 \text{ rad.} = 30^o$$

When the line-2 is suddenly switched out the rotor angle can not change instantaneously but the operating point drops to the power-angle curve corresponding to line-2 switched out case. The generator accelerates during the fault from angle δ_1 to power angle δ_i as shown in Fig. 5.31 because the output is less than the input during this period. The angle δ_i is given by the equation

$$P_i = P_{m3} \sin \delta_i$$

or $$1.5 = 2 \sin \delta_i$$

or $$\delta_i = \sin^{-1} (1.5/2) = 0.848 \text{ rad.}$$

The accelerating area

$$A_1 = \int_{\delta_1}^{\delta_i} (P_i - P_{m3} \sin \delta)\, d\delta = \int_{0.524}^{0.848} (1.5 - 2 \sin \delta)\, d\delta$$

$$= [1.5\delta + 2 \cos \delta]_{0.524}^{0.848}$$

$= (1.272 - 0.786) + 2\,(\cos 0.848 - \cos 0.524)$

$= 0.486 + (-0.409)$

$= 0.077$

For stability the rotor may swing from δ_i upto the maximum angle δ_m where $\delta_m = \pi - \delta_i = \pi - 0.848 = 2.294$ rad. $= 131.4°$.

The rotor decelerates from δ_i to maximum possible swing angle δ_m. The maximum available decelerating area $A_{2,\,\max}$ is given by

$$A_{2,\,\max} = \int_{\delta_i}^{\delta_m} (P_{m3} \sin \delta - P_i)\, d\delta = \int_{0.848}^{2.294} (2 \sin \delta - 1.5)\, d\delta$$

$= [-2 \cos \delta - 1.5\delta]_{0.848}^{2.294}$

$= -2\,(\cos 2.294 - \cos 0.848) - 1.5\,(2.294 - 0.848)$

$= 2.647 - 2.169$

$= 0.478$

Since $A_{2,\,\max} > A_1$ therefore the system is stable. The maximum rotor swing δ_2 is less than δ_m and can be obtained by equating area A_1 to area A_2 where area A_2 is given by

$$A_2 = \int_{\delta_i}^{\delta_2} (P_{m3} \sin \delta - P_i)\, d\delta = \int_{0.848}^{\delta_2} (2 \sin \delta - 1.5)\, d\delta$$

$= [-2 \cos \delta - 1.5\delta]_{0.848}^{\delta_2}$

$= -2\,(\cos \delta_2 - \cos 0.848) - 1.5\,(\delta_2 - 0.848)$

$= 2.595 - 2 \cos \delta_2 - 1.5\delta_2$

Equating the areas A_1 and A_2 gives

$$0.077 = 2.595 - 2 \cos \delta_2 - 1.5\delta_2$$

or $$2 \cos \delta_2 + 1.5\delta_2 = 2.518$$

The equation is non-linear in terms of δ_2 therefore can be solved by iterative method. By iterative solution one may get maximum rotor swing $\delta_2 = 1.218$ rad. $= 69.8°$.

Example 5.10. A generator operating with constant excitation is supplying 50 MW power to an infinite bus. The steady state limit of the system is 100 MW. Estimate the maxinum permissible sudden increase in generator input without causing instability.

Solution : The maximum power that can be transferred $P_m = 100$ MW.

Therefore power angle curve of the system is given by

$$P = P_m \sin \delta$$

or $$P = 100 \sin \delta$$

The power angle curve of the system is shown in Fig. 5.32.

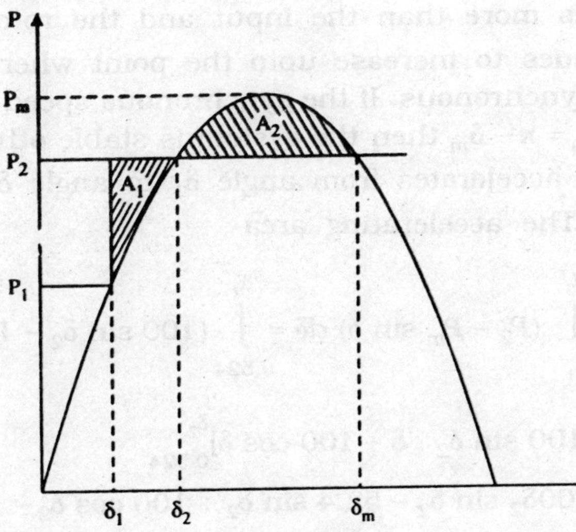

Fig. 5.32

As the system is in equilibrium before sudden increase in generator input therefore the initial mechanical input to the generator P_1 is equal to the power supplied to the infinite bus. Therefore

$$P_1 = 50 \text{ MW}$$

The power angle δ_1 before the sudden increase in generator input is given by the equation

$$P_1 = P_m \sin \delta_1$$

or $$50 = 100 \sin \delta_1$$

or $\delta_1 = \sin^{-1}(100/2) = 0.524$ rad. $= 30^\circ$

Let the maximum permissible suddenly increased input be P_2 and the operating angle corresponding to this input in steady state be δ_2 then

$$P_2 = P_m \sin\delta_2 = 100 \sin\delta_2$$

As soon as the generator input is suddenly increased the rotor angle can not change instantaneously and therefore the input becomes more than the output causing acceleration of the rotor. Therefore the rotor speed and the rotor angle increase. At rotor angle δ_2 the output becomes equal to the input causing accelerating power to become zero but the rotor angle continues to increase as rotor has already acquired speed more than synchronous which can not drop suddenly to synchronous. As the rotor angle increases beyond δ_2 the output becomes more than the input and the rotor decelerates but the rotor angle continues to increase upto the point where the rotor speed becomes equal to the synchronous. If the synchronous speed is acquired before the maximum angle $\delta_m = \pi - \delta_m$ then the system is stable otherwise the system is unstable. The rotor accelerates from angle δ_1 to angle δ_2 and decelerates from angle δ_2 to δ_m. The accelerating area

$$A_1 = \int_{\delta_1}^{\delta_2} (P_2 - P_m \sin\delta)\, d\delta = \int_{0.524}^{\delta_2} (100 \sin\delta_2 - 100 \sin\delta)\, d\delta$$

$$= [100 \sin\delta_2 \,.\, \delta + 100 \cos\delta]_{0.524}^{\delta_2}$$

$$= 100\delta_2 \sin\delta_2 - 52.4 \sin\delta_2 + 100 \cos\delta_2 - 100 \cos 0.524$$

For stability the rotor may swing from δ_2 upto the maximum angle δ_m where $\delta_m = \pi - \delta_2$. The rotor decelerates from δ_2 to maximum possible swing angle δ_m. The maximum available decelerating area $A_{2.\,max}$ is given by

$$A_{2.\,max} = \int_{\delta_2}^{\delta_m} (P_m \sin\delta - P_2)\, d\delta = \int_{\delta_2}^{\pi - \delta_2} (100 \sin\delta - 100 \sin\delta_2)\, d\delta$$

$$= [-100 \cos\delta - 100 \sin\delta_2 \,.\, \delta]_{\delta_2}^{\pi - \delta_2}$$

$$= -100\,[\cos(\pi - \delta_2) - \cos\delta_2] - 100 \sin\delta_2\,(\pi - \delta_2 - \delta_2)$$

$$= -100\,[-\cos\delta_2 - \cos\delta_2] - 100 \sin\delta_2\,(\pi - 2\delta_2)$$

$$= 200 \cos \delta_2 - 100 \sin \delta_2 (\pi - 2\delta_2).$$

For stability

Area A_1 = Area $A_{2,\, max}$

or $\quad 100\, \delta_2 \sin \delta_2 - 52.4 \sin \delta_2 + 100 \cos \delta_2 - 100 \cos 0.524$

$$= 200 \cos \delta_2 - 100 \sin \delta_2 (\pi - 2\delta_2)$$

or $\quad \delta_2 \sin \delta_2 (100 - 200) - \sin \delta_2 (52.4 - 100\pi)$

$$+ \cos \delta_2 (100 - 200) - 100 \cos 0.524 = 0$$

or $$- 100\delta_2 \sin \delta_2 + 261.8 \sin \delta_2 - 100 \cos \delta_2 - 100 \cos 0.524 = 0$$

or $$\sin \delta_2 (261.8 - 100\delta_2) - 100 \cos \delta_2 - 86.6 = 0$$

Solving the expression one may get $\delta_2 = 1.0472$ rad $= 60°$.

Therefore maximum increased input

$$P_2 = P_m \sin \delta_2 = 100 \sin 60°$$

$$= 86.6 \text{ MW}$$

Therefore sudden increase in input

$$= P_2 - P_1 = 86.6 - 50$$

$$= 36.6 \text{ MW}.$$

Example 5.11. A synchronous motor of negligible resistance is receiving 25% of power that it is capable of receiving from infinite bus. If the load on the motor is suddenly doubled, calculate the maximum value of power angle δ during the swinging of the motor around its new equilibrium position.

Solution : Let the maximum power which can be received by the motor $= P_m$

Therefore electrical power input P_e to the motor is given by

$$P_e = P_m \sin \delta$$

where δ is the power angle and is equal to the phase angle difference between the infinite bus voltage and voltage generated by motor excitation.

Given that electrical power input to motor $P_e = 0.25 P_m$. At this input let the power angle δ be equal to δ_1. Then

$$P_e = 0.25P_m = P_m \sin \delta_1$$

or $$\delta_1 = \sin^{-1} 0.25 = 0.253 \text{ rad.} = 14.48^\circ$$

The power angle curve of the motor is shown in Fig. 5.33.

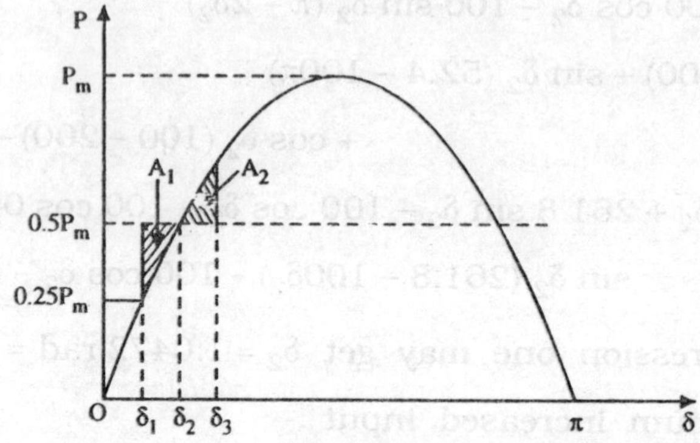

Fig. 5.33

When the load on the motor is suddenly doubled then the new load is $2 \times 0.25P_m = 0.5P_m$. In the new equilibrium position the electrical input will be equal to the load *i.e.*, $P_e = 0.5P_m$ and if the power angle at this load (input) be δ_2 then

$$0.5P_m = P_m \sin \delta_2$$

or $$\delta_2 = \sin^{-1} 0.5 = 0.524 \text{ rad.} = 30^\circ$$

Let the maximum power angle during transient period be δ_3 as shown in Fig. 5.33. The rotor of motor decelerates from angle δ_1 to angle δ_2 because the electrical input is less then the load during this period. The rotor accelerates during the period from δ_2 to δ_3 because the electrical input is more than the load during this period. The maximum power angle δ_3 can be calculated by equating the decelerating area A_1 and accelerating area A_2 shown in Fig. 5.33. Now decelerating area

$$A_1 = \int_{\delta_1}^{\delta_2} (0.5P_m - P_m \sin \delta)\, d\delta = \int_{0.253}^{0.524} (0.5P_m - P_m \sin \delta)\, d\delta$$

$$= [0.5P_m + P_m \cos \delta]_{0.253}^{0.524}$$

$$= 0.5P_m (0.524 - 0.253) + P_m (\cos 0.524 - \cos 0.253)$$

$$= 0.1355P_m - 0.1023P_m = 0.0332P_m$$

and accelerating area

$$A_2 = \int_{\delta_2}^{\delta_3} (P_m \sin \delta - 0.5P_m)\, d\delta = \int_{0.524}^{\delta_3} (P_m \sin \delta - 0.5P_m)\, d\delta$$

$$= [-P_m \cos \delta - 0.5P_m \delta]_{0.524}^{\delta_3}$$

$$= -P_m (\cos \delta_3 - \cos 0.524) - 0.5P_m (\delta_3 - 0.524)$$

$$= P_m \cos 0.524 + 0.5 \times 0.524P_m - P_m \cos \delta_3 - 0.5P_m \delta_3$$

$$= 1.1278P_m - P_m \cos \delta_3 - 0.5P_m \delta_3$$

Equating the areas A_1 and A_2 gives

$$0.0332P_m = 1.1278P_m - P_m \cos \delta_3 - 0.5P_m \delta_3$$

or $$\cos \delta_3 + 0.5\delta_3 = 1.0946$$

The equation is non-linear in terms of δ_3 therefore can be solved by iterative method. By iterative solution one may get maximum rotor swing

$$\delta_3 = 0.81 \text{ rad.} = 46.4^\circ.$$

5.9 APPLICATION OF EQUAL AREA CRITERION FOR TWO FINITE MACHINES CASE

A system having two finite machines may be replaced by an equivalent system having one finite machine and one infinite bus, so that the swing equations and swing curves of angular displacement between the two machines are same for both systems. It is necessary to use equivalent inertia constant, equivalent input, and equivalent output for the equivalent finite machine.

The swing equations of the two finite machines are as follows :

$$\frac{d^2\delta_1}{dt^2} = \frac{P_{a1}}{M_1} = \frac{P_{i1} - P_{e1}}{M_1}$$

and $$\frac{d^2\delta_2}{dt^2} = \frac{P_{a2}}{M_2} = \frac{P_{i2} - P_{e2}}{M_2}.$$

The relative angle between them is $\delta = \delta_1 - \delta_2$ which decides the stability of the system. Now

$$\frac{d^2\delta}{dt^2} = \frac{d^2\,\delta_1}{dt^2} - \frac{d^2\,\delta_2}{dt^2} = \frac{P_{a1}}{M_1} - \frac{P_{a2}}{M_2}$$

or
$$\frac{d^2\delta}{dt^2} = \frac{M_2\,P_{a1} - M_1\,P_{a2}}{M_1\,.\,M_2}$$

Multiplying both the sides by $\dfrac{M_1\,M_2}{M_1 + M_2}$ gives

or
$$\frac{M_1\,M_2}{M_1 + M_2}\,\frac{d^2\delta}{dt^2} = \frac{M_2\,P_{a1} - M_1\,P_{a2}}{M_1 + M_2}$$

$$= \frac{M_2\,P_{i1} - M_1\,P_{i2}}{M_1 + M_2} - \frac{M_2\,P_{e1} - M_1\,P_{e2}}{M_1 + M_2}$$

which may be written more simply as

$$M\frac{d^2\delta}{dt^2} = P_a = P_i - P_e$$

which is identical with the equation for single finite machine and an infinite bus. Here the equivalent input P_i, the equivalent output P_e and the equivalent inertia M are given by

$$P_i = \frac{M_2\,P_{i1} - M_1\,P_{i2}}{M_1 + M_2}$$

$$P_e = \frac{M_2\,P_{e1} - M_1\,P_{e2}}{M_1 + M_2}$$

$$M = \frac{M_1\,M_2}{M_1 + M_2}$$

This approach can also be used for a system having large number of machines. The machines are divided into two groups such that in each group all the machines swing together. Each group is converted into single equivalent machine by considering them as running in parallel and then the two group system is converted to one finite machine and one infinite bus system as above.

5.10 FACTORS AFFECTING STABILITY

The factors affecting steady state stability and transient stability are discussed separately in following sections.

5.10.1 Steady State Stability

The steady state stability is given by $P = \frac{|E|\ |V|}{X}$. Therefore following factors affect the steady state stability :

1. The excitation voltage proportional to $|E|$ affects the steady state stability limit. Higher the excitation voltage higher will be the steady state stability limit.
2. The steady state stability limit also depends upon the reactance X between generator and load, or between generators. Lower reactance causes the limit to be more. The reactance also includes the generator steady state reactances. Hence these reactances also affect the steady state stability limit. However the generator reactances are usually very small as compared with the reactance of the network.
3. The series capacitors also affect the steady state stability limit as it reduces the reactance X of the network. The series capacitors increase the steady state stability limit, in general.
4. The shunt capacitors also affect the steady state stability limit as it affects the receiving end voltage $|V|$. The shunt capacitors increase the steady state stability limit, in general.

5.10.2 Transient Stability Limit

The following factors affect the transient stability limit :

1. The reactances during fault conditions and after fault conditions affect the limit at very great extent. If the reactances during the fault condition and post-fault conditions are lower, the transient stability limit will be higher. However, for accelerating power to be lower during fault and post fault conditions it is necessary that the difference in amplitudes of the power angle curves of during fault and post-fault from pre-fault power angle curve should be small. Lower accelerating power means higher transient stability limit therefore for higher transient stability limit the reactance between generators and/or load should be higher.
2. By increasing excitation the amplitude of all the three power-angle curves;

namely prefault, during fault and post fault, increase. Therefore higher excitation results in higher transient stability limit.

3. The inertia constant also affects the transient stability limit. Higher inertia machine has more clearing time for the same fault clearing angle. Hence higher inertia machine has more transient stability limit for the same clearing time because it will have smaller clearing angle.
4. The location and type of fault affect the transient stability limit. If location and type of fault is such that the reactance between generators during fault is lower then the transient stability will be higher
5. The fast operating protective gear reduces fault clearing time and hence fault clearing angle. The lower fault clearing angle improves (increases) transient stability limit.
6. The method of connection of HV buses affects transient stability. Consider the additional links shown by dashed lines in Fig. 5.34.

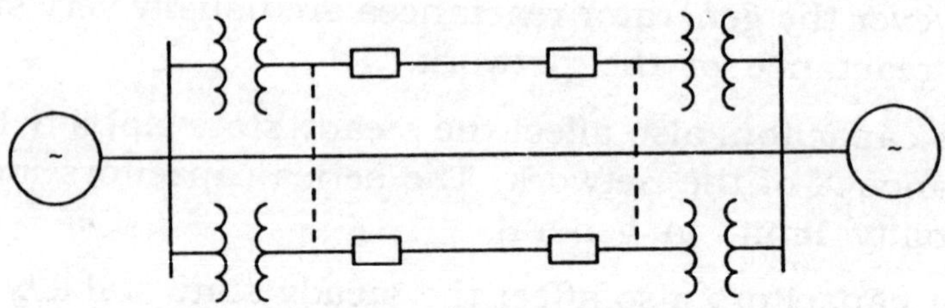

Fig. 5.34 : Method of connection of HV bus bars

In the post fault conditions both the transformers at each end shall remain still in circuit and hence overall reactance between machines reduces resulting in higher power transfer between them during this period. This improves transient stability limit. However, during fault conditions both the transformers carry the fault current in this case, which may damage the transformers. The limit can be improved without this disadvantage if fast operating protective gears are in circuit.

If series capacitors are inserted into the circuit during fault, the reactance between machines reduces and hence it improves the transient stability limit. The shunt capacitors also affect the transient stability limit.

Single line to ground faults are more common. If single pole opening and reclosing is applied then it improves the transient stability limit. The single pole opening and reclosing is sufficient to clear a fault as in many cases the fault is not of permanent nature. This arrangement is however not very simple and is expensive.

9. If during the fault resistances are connected across generators, the transient stability improves. The resistances, called braking resistors, reduce the accelerating power during the fault period.
10. Current limiting reactors improve the transient stability limit. These improve the voltages during the fault conditions thereby improving the load level and reducing the difference in mechanical input and electrical output of generators.
11. When a fault occurs on a system the voltages at all buses are reduced. At generator terminals the reduced voltages are sensed by the automatic voltage regulators which act within the excitation system to restore generator terminal voltages. The general effect of the excitation system is to increase amplitude of during fault power-angle curve which reduces the initial rotor angle swing following the fault and improves transient stability limit. Therefore fast acting excitation systems improve transient stability limit.
12. Modern turbine governing systems have the ability to close turbine valves to reduce acceleration during fault. Immediately upon detecting difference between mechanical input and electrical output, control action initiates the valve closing which reduces mechanical power input and accelerating power. Fast valving improves transient stability limit.
13. Recent trends in design of large alternators tend toward lower short circuit ratio (SCR = $1/X_d$), which is achieved by reducing machine air gap with consequent saving in machine mmf, size, weight and cost. Reduction in the size of rotor reduces inertia constant, lowering thereby the stability limit. Thus lower SCR reduces transient stability limit. The loss in stability limit is made up by faster circuit breakers, faster excitation systems and fast valving.
14. The operating frequency of the system also affects the transient stability limit. At lower frequency the reactances are lower therefore transient stability limit is higher.

5.11 POWER SYSTEM SECURITY

Present day power systems are large and complex. With the current rise in demand of electrical energy, power systems will continue to grow both in size and complexity. Our dependence on electricity is too much at the present time and it is increasing day by day. Therefore, it is essential to have uninterrupted (reliable) supply of electrical power within set limits of frequency and voltage levels. Due to economic reasons and uncertainties in the forecast of loads and in the completion dates of new facilities, power supply reliability does not attain 100-percent level. The building of extra high voltage tie lines has resulted in further propagation of the effects of disturbances.

Initially power system control was dedicated to the generation and economic operation but with the increased emphasis on the security a new dimension in power system operation has been added which is much broader in scope of system monitoring and control. Large blackouts in the 1960's, such as the Northeast blackout in the U.S.A., stimulated the study of security control of electric power systems. Consequently, the burden on the system operators to ensure the operation of power systems to meet the above requirements has increased tremendously. Therefore, it becomes a necessity to develop methods for effective control and secure operation of power systems.

The various states in which a power system operates can be classified into the following three states :

1. **Normal operating state** : When an operating state of a power system fulfills load demand at acceptable level of voltage and frequency without violating ratings of generators and transmission equipment then the state of power system is said to be a normal operating state.

2. **Emergency operating state** : When an operating state of power system is such that the system loads are met but
   (*a*) some system components are overloaded, or
   (*b*) the specified quality of the supply can not be maintained, or
   (*c*) the system is in the process of losing synchronism, then the state of the system is said to be in emergency operating state.

3. **Restorative operating state** : When the power system is not able to fulfill the system load demand but is operating in such a way that all other constraints such as constraints on voltage, frequency and power flows through generators and transmission equipment are satisfied, then the state of the system is called restorative operating state. This normally occurs after an emergency during which the supply to some customers has been curtailed.

It is the aim of the operators to maintain the system in the normal operating state even unuer foreseeable circumstances. Controls chosen by the operator to achieve this aim are thus preventive in nature.

In practice, it is not sufficient just to maintain a system in normal operating state. Under normal operation of power systems, there may occur faults or other disturbances which have the potential of shifting the operating point. At the new operating point the power system may be in normal operating state or it may be in an undesirable emergency state. In this framework, the security of the power system is defined. A set of most probable disturbances (contingencies) is first specified. Suppose that a power system in the normal operating state is subjected to the set of disturbances one at a time. If after occurrence of every single disturbance in the specified set, the system remains normal, then the predisturbance or prefault state of the system is said to be a secure state. Otherwise, it is an insecure state.

The power system security may be divided into three modes, namely :

(*a*) steady state security which deals with the steady state conditions of a system,

(*b*) transient security which concerns the transient stability of a system when it is subjected to a disturbance, and

(*c*) dynamic security which pertains to the system responses of the order of a few minutes.

Power system operating state is never static as the system load demand is always changing. Thus some kind of security assessment must be undertaken from time to time, and corrective actions taken in case system is in insecure state. Preferably, this should be done alongwith economic dispatch calculations.

REVIEW QUESTIONS

5.1 Define and explain the meaning of power system stability.

5.2 Define steady state, transient and dynamic stabilities.

5.3 Distinguish between steady state, transient and dynamic stability of a power system.

5.4 Define the steady state stability limit of a transmission line. Derive an expression for the steady state stability limit of a transmission line connecting two machines.

5.5 Define and explain transient stability limit of a transmission line.

5.6 Obtain the equivalent circuit representation of synchronous machines in steady state.

5.7 Obtain the equivalent circuit representation of synchronous machines in transient state.

5.8 Define inertia constant and derive its relationship with angular momentum. Why is inertia constant widely used?

5.9 Derive an expression for equivalent inertia constant of several synchronous machines connected in parallel at one point.

5.10 Starting from first principles, derive the swing equation of a synchronous machine.

5.11 Explain the concept of equal area criterion. How can it be used to study transient stability?

5.12 Explain the application of equal area criterion to study transient stability for the following cases :

(*a*) A sustained line fault

(*b*) A line fault cleared after the lapse of a certain time by the simultaneous opening of the circuit breakers at both ends of the line.

(*c*) Case (*b*) followed by reclosing.

5.13 Explain the application of equal area criterion for two finite machines case.

5.14 Discuss the factors affecting steady state stability.

5.15 Discuss the factors affecting transient stability.

5.16 Define normal operating state, emergency operating state and restorative operating state of power system.

5.17 Define security of power system. Distinguish between steady state, transient and dynamic security of a power system.

Chapter 6

EXTRA HIGH VOLTAGE TRANSMISSION

Transmission of electrical power at extra high voltages (voltages beyond 300 kV) has become a necessity in modern power systems. The transmission lines energised at extra high voltages produce high electrostatic fields which is dangerous and harmful to the human beings, animals and plants. At high voltages corona loss becomes predominant, specially in bad weather, and needs to be given importance in design of the extra high voltage lines. The high voltage lines also produce radio noise which interfere with the nearby other services. To limit the corona loss and radio noise the extra high voltage lines generally use bundled conductor. Beyond a certain distance, the transmission of electrical power on high voltage DC becomes economical as compared with transmission at extra high voltage AC. But if the distance is too large then AC transmission on tuned lines becomes economical.

6.1 NEED FOR EXTRA HIGH VOLTAGE (EHV) TRANSMISSION

Transmission of electrical power at extra high voltages (EHV) is needed due to the following reasons :

1. **Increase in size of generating units** : In order to reduce the investment cost per kW, the size of generating units has been constantly increased during the past many years. Transmission of large amounts of power is technically and economically feasible only at voltages in the extra high voltage range.
2. **Pithead steam plants and remote hydro plants** : The cost of transportation is an appreciable part of the cost of coal, especially for regions situated far away from coal fields. Sometimes the bottle-necks in transportation tend to reduce supply of coal to steam plants resulting in fall of generation.

One method to avoid such situations is to have super thermal power plants near coal fields. These steam plants are known as pithead steam plants. Therefore now the trend is towards construction of large sized pithead steam plants which has resulted in transmission of bulk power over long distances. Similarly the hydro plants are usually situated far away from the load centres because the availability of water at sufficient head is only at remote locations. Therefore EHV transmission systems are needed to transmit the large amounts of power over long distances from the pithead steam plants and remote hydro plants to load centres.

3. **Right-of-way problem** : The number of circuits and consequently the land requirement for transmission lines decreases with the adoption of a higher transmission voltage. For transmitting 600 MW over a distance of 250 kms requires 40 m right-of-way at 400 kv level using single circuit line and 60 m right-of-way at 220 kv level using double circuit line. Thus the savings in right-of-way and subsequently its cost at EHV level may be substantial.
4. **Line costs** : The line installation cost per MW per km decreases with increase in voltage level. The transmission losses and hence cost of losses decreases with increase in transmission voltage. Therefore the total line cost, including the cost of losses, per MW per km decreases considerably with the increase in line voltage.
5. **Loading limit** : The loading limit of a line is closely related with its surge impedance loading (SIL). The surge impedance loading is the load that a line carries when each phase is terminated by a load equal to the surge impedance of the line. A short transmission line can be loaded appreciably above its SIL. However, the load on a long line without series compensation has to be kept at a value less than the SIL due to stability considerations. Series compensation may be used to increase line loading limit whenever the series compensation is more economical than the use of additional lines or going to next higher voltage. In all cases, the surge impedance loading represents the approximate load carrying capability of lines. The surge impedance loading equals V^2/Z_c where V is the line to line voltage and Z_c is the surge impedance. The surge impedance is independent of voltage level and depends only on the conductor configuration. The approximate values of surge impedance for lines with single, double, triple and quadruple conductors are 400, 300, 280 and 260 ohms. Therefore the surge impedance loading and hence the loading limit of transmission line is proportional to square of the transmission voltage. It is therefore

evident that as line loads increase, a stage comes when it is necessary to adopt a higher voltage.

6.2 SURGE IMPEDANCE LOADING

Surge impedance loading (SIL) is the load that a line carries when each phase is terminated by a load equal to the surge impedance of the line. Surge impedance Z_c of a line is numerically equal to $\sqrt{(L/C)}$ where L is the series inductance per unit length and C is the shunt capacitance per unit length. If V is the line to neutral voltage, SIL equals $3V^2/Z_c$. At this loading the reactive power consumed by the line inductance ωLI^2 is approximately equal to the reactive power generated by the line capacitance ωCV^2. The transient stability limit of a line is closely related with the SIL of a line. Transient stability considerations require that the phase angle across a line should be less than 30°. The maximum load, in terms of surge impedance loading, that can be carried through an uncompensated line is given in Fig. 6.1.

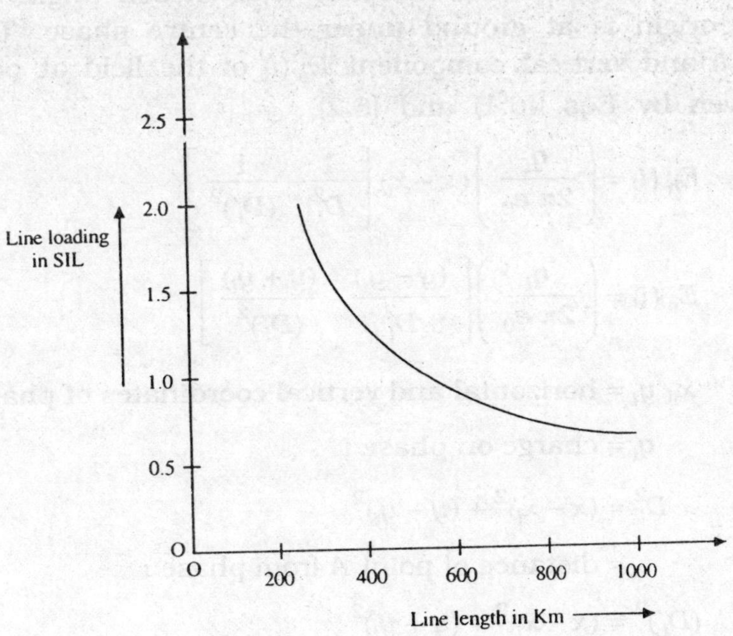

Fig. 6.1 : Loading of lines without series compensation

6.3 ELECTROSTATIC FIELDS OF EHV LINES

EHV lines produce high electrostatic fields under them which cause damage to human life, animals and plants. Experiments have shown that the human beings may experience a shock if the electrostatic field produced by EHV lines exceeds 15 kv/m rms. The animals are affected by high electrostatic field at about 30 kv/m rms. The plants are affected at a field strength of 20 kv/m rms. Therefore an EHV line must be designed such that the electrostatic field at ground level does not exceed 15 kv/m rms.

Vehicles parked under an EHV line or driving through acquire electrostatic charge if their tyres are made of insulating material. If parking lots are located under a line, the minimum recommended safe clearance is 17 m for 345 kv and 20 m for 400 kv lines. Trucks and lorries require an extra 3 m clearance. The electrostatic charge produced by electrostatic field of EHV line may be dangerous when a human being in the vehicle opens the door and gets a shock.

To calculate the electrostatic field of EHV lines the horizontal and vertical components of the field are determined at the required point $A\,(x, y)$ where x and y are its coordinates with reference to a chosen origin. A convenient location of the origin is at ground under the centre phase. The horizontal component $E_h\,(i)$ and vertical component $E_v\,(i)$ of the field at point A due to phase i are given by Eqs. (6.1) and (6.2).

$$E_h\,(i) = \left(\frac{q_i}{2\pi\, e_0}\right)(x - x_i)\left[\frac{1}{D_i^2} - \frac{1}{(D_i')^2}\right] \qquad \text{...(6.1)}$$

and

$$E_v\,(i) = \left(\frac{q_i}{2\pi\, e_0}\right)\left[\frac{(y - y_i)}{D_i^2} - \frac{(y + y_i)}{(D_i')^2}\right] \qquad \text{...(6.2)}$$

x_i, y_i = horizontal and vertical coordinates of phase i

q_i = charge on phase i

$D_i^2 = (x - x_i)^2 + (y - y_i)^2$

= distance of point A from phase i

$(D_i')^2 = (x - x_i)^2 + (y + y_i)^2$

= distance of point A from image of phase i

Due to all the phases i = 1, 2, ..., n the sum of horizontal components E_{hn} and vertical components E_{vn} of electrostatic field at the point $A\,(x\ y)$ will be

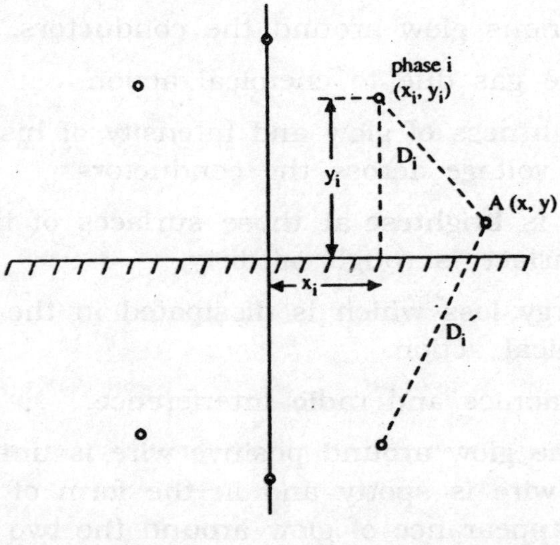

Fig. 6.2 : Electrostatic field of EHV lines

$$E_{hn} = \sum_{i=1}^{n} E_h(i) \qquad \text{...(6.3)}$$

$$E_{vn} = \sum_{i=1}^{n} E_v(i) \qquad \text{...(6.4)}$$

The total electric field E_{tn} at point A is

$$E_{tn} = (E_{hn}^2 + E_{vn}^2)^{0.5} \qquad \text{...(6.5)}$$

$$= [(\Sigma E_h(i))^2 + (\Sigma E_v(i))^2]^{0.5} \qquad \text{...(6.6)}$$

If H_i be the height of conductor above ground then y_i can be taken equal to H_i in the expression given by Eq. (6.2).

6.4 CORONA EFFECT

Corona is the local breakdown of air in the immediate vicinity of the conductors. When the diameter of the conductors is very small as compared with the spacing between them then the voltage gradient at the surface of the conductors is highest and may exceed the breakdown strength of the air causing local breakdown of air and so the corona results. The corona has following effects :

1. It produces localized breakdown around the conductors.

2. It produces hissing sound.
3. It produces luminous glow around the conductors.
4. It produces ozone gas due to chemical action.
5. The size and brightness of glow and intensity of hissing sound increase with increase in voltage across the conductors
6. The corona glow is brightest at those surfaces of the conductor where the conductor surface is rough or dirty.
7. It results in energy loss which is dissipated in the form of heat, light, sound and chemical action.
8. It generates harmonics and radio interference.
9. In case of d.c. the glow around positive wire is uniform while the glow around negative wire is spotty and in the form of short streamers. In the case of a.c. appearance of glow around the two conductors is same since the conductors are alternately positive and negative.

6.5 CORONA LOSS

In general the magnitude of fair weather corona loss is generally small for most of the EHV lines. However some designers consider it to be economically significant because the fair weather loss exists for a very large percentage of total operating time. The corona loss in fair weather can be calculated using Peeks or Peterson's formula. The corona loss under bad weather conditions may be as high as 100 times the fair weather corona loss. However, the bad weather persists for only a short time during the year.

For estimating the corona loss during bad weather (rainy season) for EHV lines, the following formula can be used :

$$\Sigma P = P_{fw} + \left[\frac{V}{1.6} Jr^2 \ln (1 + 10R) \right] \sum_{i}^{n} (E^5) \quad ...(6.7)$$

where ΣP = total 3 phase corona loss, kW per 3 phase km

P_{fw} = total fair weather corona loss, kW per 3 phase km.

(can be calculated using Peek's or Peterson's formula)

V = line to neutral voltage, kV

$J = 7.04 \times 10^{-10}$ for 400 kV lines

$= 5.35 \times 10^{-10}$ for 500 kV and 765 kV lines

r = sub-conductor radius, cms.

n = total number of sub-conductors (*i.e.*, number of sub conductor per hundle × 3)

E = gradient at the bottom of each sub-conductors, kV peak/cm.

R = rain rate in mm per hour.

Through the use of the factor $\sum_{1}^{n} E^5$ the gradient at the bottom of each conductor is calculated individually and raised to the power 5 and then summation is done for all the sub-conductors. Eq. (6.7) can also be used for calculating corona loss under conditions of snow and frost. The value of J should be taken as 1.27×10^{-9} for snow and frost conditions and the following equivalent rain rates may be used for these conditions.

For heavy snow $R = 2.54$ mm per hour

For medium snow $R = 0.636$ mm per hour

For light snow $R = 0.0127$ mm per hour

For calculating the total corona loss of a line for one year the hour to hour corona loss for the total duration is calculated by including the meteorological conditions at different times during the year and then added.

6.6 RADIO NOISE FROM EHV LINES

The radio noise, also called as radio interference, originates from the same source as the corona *i.e.*, the localized breakdown. The radio interference field generated from transmission line varies mostly as the inverse of the radio frequency. Thus services in the higher frequency band (television, frequency modulated broadcasting, radar, microwave relay stations etc.) are less likely to be affected. The directional antenna which are generally used at these frequencies increase the signal to noise ratio. Much radio interference is caused to home and automobile radio receivers operating in the amplitude modulation broadcast frequencies, power line carrier communication, low frequency aviation, marine and other similar services.

The radio interference due to corona assumes importance for lines above 200 kV. For EHV lines the line design is affected to a large extent by this phenomenon. Since radio noise is associated with corona it is mainly dependent on the potential gradients at the conductors. However, it is also influenced by all the other factors which influence corona, such as air density, humidity, wind contaminants, imperfections and precipitation. The exact calculation of radio noise from a line is a difficult exercise so computer programs have been developed for this purpose. As an alternative some empirical formulae have also been developed. One of these is

$$RN = 50 + K(E_m - 16.95) + 40 \log \frac{d}{3.93} + F_n + 32 \log \frac{20}{R} + F_{fw}$$

where, RN = radio noise in dB above 1 μV/m at 1 MHz

K = 3 for 750 kV class

= 3.5 for others, gradient limits 15 – 19 kV/cm

E_m = maximum electric field at conductor, kV-rms/cm

d = sub-conductor diameter, cm

F_n = – 4 for single conductor

= 10 log (n/4), for $n > 1$

n = number of sub-conductors in a bundle

R = distance from line, m

F_{fw} = 17 for bad weather and zero for fair weather.

In determining *RI* (radio interference) performance of a proposed line the magnitude of *RI* factors for the entire frequency range of communication sources has to be evaluated. To calculate radio noise for other frequencies the following formula is used :

$$RI \,\alpha\, \frac{1}{f} \text{ or } RI \,\alpha\, \frac{1}{f^{1.5}}$$

where f is the frequency and *RI* is radio interference. Thus, at 0.5 MHz the radio noise is 6 to 9 dB higher than at 1 MHz, while at 2 MHz it is 6-9 dB lower. To calculate radio noise *RN* at any frequency f' MHz following formula may be used :

$$RN_{f'} = (RN \text{ at 1 MHz in dB}) + 20 \log (1/f')$$

For good radio reception, the desired signal level should be 20 to 25 dB over the noise level. If radio interference is particularly troublesome for few selective frequencies at some locations, selective filters can be installed on the lines to suppress these frequencies. A quarter wave trap has been used successfully in USA. This is an open ended line section, one quarter wavelength long, connected in shunt with the line. The effect is to place a short circuit on the line for the frequencies to be filtered.

The design of EHV line considering *RI* is outlined as follows. The *RI* level is calculated for the proposed line configuration. If *RI* level is more than the limit then either alternate designs are considered or Right-of-way width is increased. Suitable filters may also be designed and proposed if *RI* level is higher for a few selective frequencies only.

6.7 USE OF BUNDLED CONDUCTORS

For lines upto 220 kV, the size of the conductor is selected on the basis of its continuous and short term current carrying capacity. However for EHV lines the corona and radio interference aspects also assume importance. The size of the conductor which gives satisfactory corona and radio interference performance is usually larger than the size corresponding to current carrying capacity.

If a single conductor per phase is used and the size of the conductor is selected on the basis of the current carrying capacity alone, the gradient at the surface of the conductor would often be higher than the acceptable value (between 20 – 30 kV peak per cm.). One solution is to use hollow conductors. These conductors have filler material or air spaces in the interior so that the outside diameter is increased. However due to manufacturing problem and the fact that hollow conductors must be handled very carefully to avoid deformation (which increase voltage gradient) these conductors are not used widely. The only other alternative is to use 2 or more sub-conductors per phase so as to give a lower maximum and average voltage gradient than that which a single conductor of the same conductivity would give. Such an arrangement is known as bundled conductors. The number of sub-conductors per phase can be 2, 3, 4, or even 8. The 400 kV lines use only 2 sub-conductors per phase. The 765 kV lines in USA and other countries use upto 8 sub-conductors per phase. The bundled conductors have less inductance and more capacitance compared to single conductor.

When bundled conductors are used, spacers have to be installed at intervals of 80 – 100 m in each span to maintain the spacing between the sub-conductors. This is necessary to prevent the conductors from getting stuck-up due to wind forces or electromagnetic induction introduced by heavy currents. The increase in surge impedance loading with the increase in the spacing between the sub-conductors is small and, therefore, the intrabundle spacings are not very critical and 45 cms is the most commonly used value throughout the world. The bundled conductors are subject to greater ice and wind loadings than single conductors of the same total cross-section and, therefore, require slightly stronger towers.

6.8 TUNED POWER LINES

Hydroelectric and super thermal power plants are generally located at great distances from the load centres. It is necessary to use extra long distance (ELD) point to point transmission lines for transporting electrical energy from these plants to load centres. The design of ELD lines is becoming increasingly difficult due to high cost of compensating equipment such as series capacitors. In addition to high capital cost due to compensating equipment, ELD lines produce many operating problems such as surplus vars during light load conditions, Ferranti effect, generator self excitation and large voltage drop during heavy line loadings. These problems are predominant over extra long distances of over 1000 kms. Tuned power lines provide one solution to this extra long distance power transmission problem.

6.8.1 Principle of Tuned Power Lines

The performance equations of a long transmission line of length l are

$$V_s = \cosh(\Gamma l)\, V_r + Z_c \sinh(\Gamma l)\, I_r \quad \text{...(6.8)}$$

and $$I_s = \frac{1}{Z_c} \sinh(\Gamma l)\, V_r + \cosh(\Gamma l)\, I_r \quad \text{...(6.9)}$$

where $$Z_c = \text{characteristic impedance} = \sqrt{(z/y)} \quad \text{...(6.10)}$$

$$\Gamma = \sqrt{(zy)} \quad \text{...(6.11)}$$

z, y = series impedance and shunt admittance per unit length respectively

Thus $$\Gamma = \sqrt{(r + j\omega L)\ (g + j\omega C)} \approx \sqrt{(j\omega L \,.\, j\omega C)} = j\omega\sqrt{LC} \quad \text{...(6.12)}$$

(by neglecting r and g)

The velocity of propagation υ of electrical wave is given by

$$\upsilon = (1/\sqrt{LC}) \quad \text{...(6.13)}$$

and the velocity υ, frequency f and wave length λ are related by

$$\upsilon = f\lambda \quad \text{...(6.14)}$$

From Eqs. (6.12), (6.13) and (6.14)

$$\Gamma = j\omega \frac{1}{f\lambda} = j\frac{2\pi}{\lambda} \quad \text{...(6.15)}$$

Therefore

$$\cosh(\Gamma l) = \cosh\left(j\frac{2\pi}{\lambda}l\right) = \cos(2\pi l/\lambda) \qquad ...(6.16)$$

$$\sinh(\Gamma l) = \sinh\left(j\frac{2\pi}{\lambda}l\right) = j\sin(2\pi l/\lambda) \qquad ...(6.17)$$

Substituting values from Eqs. (6.16) and (6.17) into Eqs. (6.8) and (6.9) give

$$V_s = \cos(2\pi l/\lambda)\, V_r + j Z_c \sin(2\pi l/\lambda)\, I_r \qquad ...(6.18)$$

$$I_s = \frac{j}{Z_c}\sin(2\pi l/\lambda)\, V_r + \cos(2\pi l/\lambda)\, I_r \qquad ...(6.19)$$

If $l = (\lambda/2)$ then from Eqs. (6.18) and (6.19)

$$V_s = -V_r$$

and $$I_s = -I_r$$

or $$|V_s| = |V_r| \qquad ...(6.20)$$

$$|I_s| = |I_r| \qquad ...(6.21)$$

The Eqs. (6.20) and (6.21) show that when the length of a transmission line is tuned to half wave length $\lambda/2$ then the receiving end voltage and current are numerically equal to the sending end voltage and current respectively. Thus the sending end and receiving end are virtually same. This is the principle of tuned power lines.

The salient features of tuned power lines are :

1. The general line constants for an exact tuned line are $A = D = -1$ and $B = C = 0$. This means that such a line presents zero series impedance and zero shunt admittance.
2. The receiving end voltage and current are equal in magnitude and 180° out of phase with sending end voltage and current *i.e.*, $V_r = -V_s$ and $I_r = -I_s$.
3. The line is neither a sink nor a source of vars (*i.e.*, $V_s I_s^* = V_r I_r^*$).
4. There is no ferranti effect when the line is open circuited at the receiving end.

5. The electrical length of a half wave length tuned power line is 180°.

6.8.2 Practical Considerations

The electrical length of the line (including transformation equipment) should be about 10° more than one half of a wave length due to two important reasons. The first reason is to reduce the required sensitivity of the generator var output control and the second is to ensure a half wave length transmission during temporary reduced frequency operation. As the frequency drops the wave length of electrical wave increases because wave length is inversely proportional to frequency. If a sufficient margin of safety is not provided, loss of power flow may occur. If the line is electrically lengthened so that its effective electrical length is between 180° and 270°, the system is as stable as the one operating in first quadrant *i.e.*, 0 to 90°.

6.8.3 Tuning of Transmission Lines

The length of a natural half wave length tuned line is 3000 kms for 50 Hz system. The resistance of such a long line would be very high causing large transmission losses and making the line uneconomical. Changing the line parameters such as conductor size, grouping, phase spacing etc. has practically no effect on wave length. However it is possible to increase the electrical length of an actual short line by using tuning equipment. The tuning equipment are the lumped capacitor and inductor networks. Two methods are available for this purpose. In the first method the tuning equipment is placed at the ends of the line in the form of π-sections (Fig. 6.3 (*a*)) or *T*-sections (Fig. 6.3 (*b*)). In the second method the tuning equipment comprises of shunt capacitors connected along the line at a few points (Fig. 6.3 (*c*)).

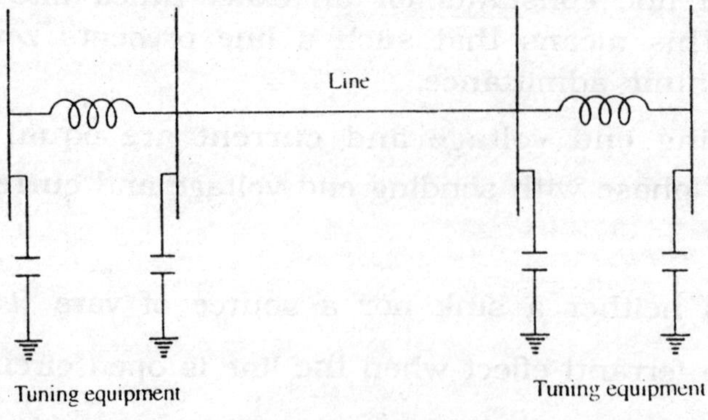

Fig. 6.3 (*a*) : π section tuning

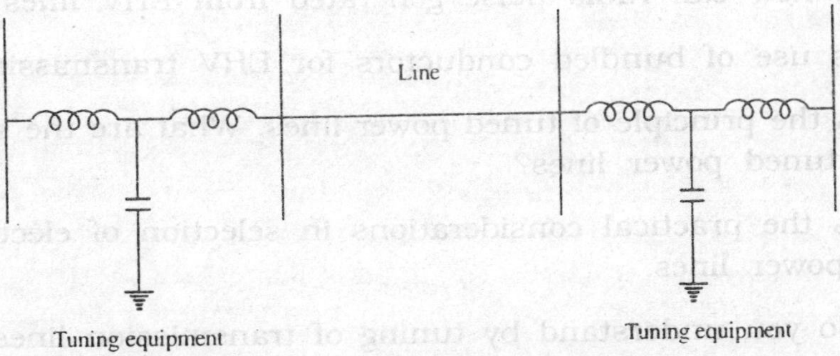

Fig. 6.3 (*b*) T-section tuning

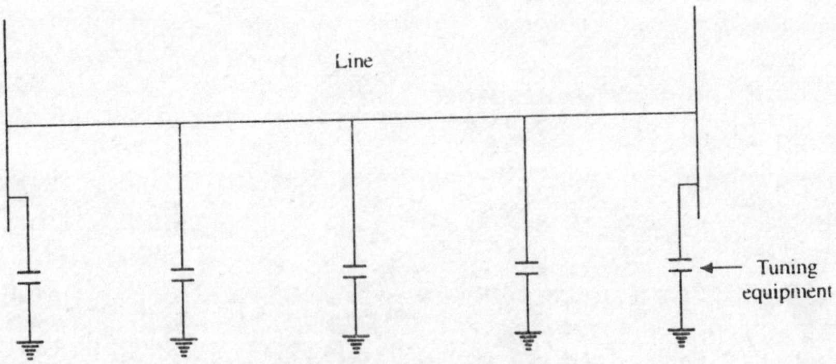

(c) Capacitance tuning

Fig. 6.3 : Tuning Equipment for power lines

REVIEW QUESTIONS

6.1 Explain why the EHV transmission is necessary in modern power systems.

6.2 Explain the relevance of surge impedance loading in Extra High Voltage Transmission.

6.3 Why estimation of electrostatic fields of EHV lines is necessary? Explain how the electrostatic fields of EHV lines can be calculated.

6.4 Discuss the effects of corona.

6.5 Discuss corona loss in EHV lines under bad weather conditions and its estimation.

6.6 Explain how can radio noise generated from EHV lines be estimated.

6.7 Discuss use of bundled conductors for EHV transmission lines.

6.8 Explain the principle of tuned power lines. What are the salient features of the tuned power lines?

6.9 Discuss the practical considerations in selection of electrical length of tuned power lines.

6.10 What do you understand by tuning of transmission lines? Discuss the various methods of tuning of transmission lines.

Chpater 7

HVDC TRANSMISSION

The first power system was operating with direct current (dc). The invention of transformer and induction motor led the alternating current (ac) power system. The ac system has the advantage of facilitating generation, transmission and distribution of electricity at different voltage levels due to transformer. However, transmission of electrical power at ac becomes infeasible through cables if the distance is more than 50 kms due to excessive charging currents. The dc transmission proved to be economical for these cases. Also when the transmission of electrical power through overhead lines is required for about more than 700 kms the EHV transmission becomes uneconomical and here high voltage direct current (HVDC) transmission proves to be economical.

The HVDC transmission lines usually connect two ac systems. At sending end ac is converted into dc by using rectifier, also called converter, and at the receiving end dc is again converted into ac by using inverters. Sometimes both the rectifier and inverter are referred to as converters. Various types of dc links for connecting ac systems through dc transmission are in use. The HVDC transmission has many advantages but at the same time few disadvantages too. A station connecting ac system to dc system, called converter station, requires many equipments apart from rectifiers and inverters. The HVDC systems usually use ground as return path. The HVDC transmission has many useful applications.

7.1 TYPES OF DC LINKS

The dc links can be classified into the following three types :

7.1.1 Monopolar Link

A monopolar link is shown in Fig. 7.1.

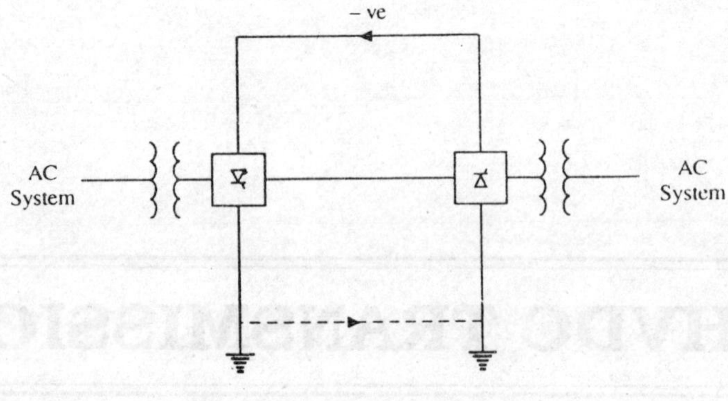

Fig. 7.1 : Monopolar link

The monopolar dc link has one conductor usually of negative polarity and uses ground or sea as return. The overhead conductor is kept at negative polarity because negative conductor has considerably less corona loss and radio interference as compared to the positive conductor. Sometimes metallic return is also used in monopolar link.

7.1.2 Bipolar Link

A bipolar link is shown in Fig. 7.2.

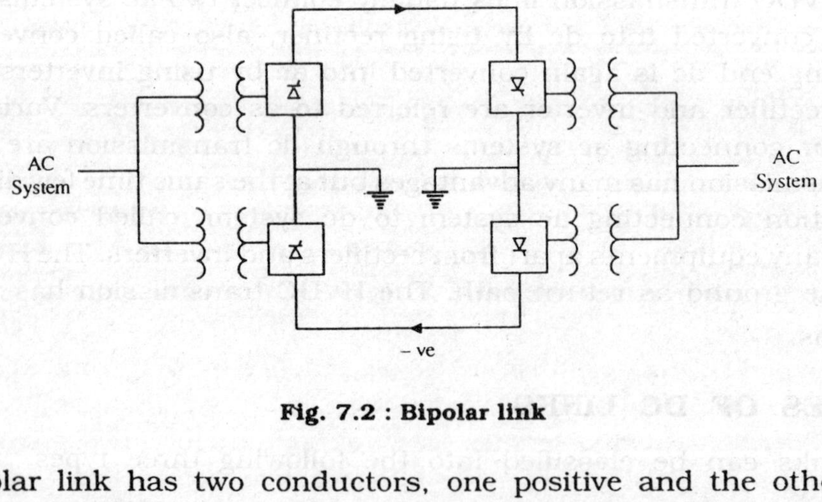

Fig. 7.2 : Bipolar link

A bipolar link has two conductors, one positive and the other negative. At each terminal of dc line, two converters of identical ratings are connected in series on dc side. The junction point of the converters are grounded at one or both ends. If the currents in the two conductors are equal, the ground current is zero. If a fault develops on one conductor, the other conductor can supply half of the rated load along with ground return. The rated voltage of a bipolar link having 500 kV voltage on overhead conductors with respect to ground is expressed as ± 500 kV.

7.1.3 Homopolar Link

A homopolar link is shown in Fig. 7.3.

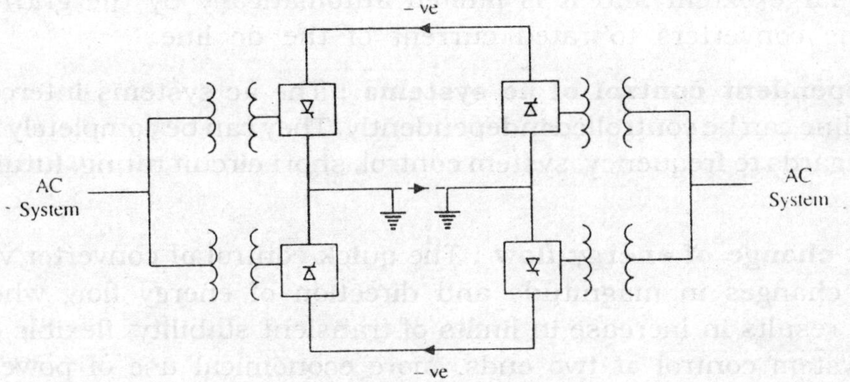

Fig. 7.3 : Homopolar link

It employs two or more conductors, all having same polarity and operated with ground or metallic return. The polarity of the conductors is usually negative as negative conductors have less corona loss and radio interference.

7.2 ADVANTAGES OF HVDC TRANSMISSION

HVDC transmission posses many advantages over ac transmission. Some of these are :

1. **Reactive power requirement** : A HVDC line neither generates nor absorbs reactive power. It also does not transmit reactive power. However the converters at the two ends draw some reactive power from ac systems for their operation. This reactive power varies with the transmitted power but is independent of line length. It is found that for lines greater than 400 km length, a dc line requires less reactive power than ac line.
2. **System stability** : Two separate ac systems interconnected by an ac line must operate with synchronism at same frequency. Two separate ac systems interconnected by a dc link may operate asynchronously and may even

operate at different frequencies. Thus HVDC gives asynchronous tie and transient stability does not pose any limit on the amount of power which can be transmitted through it. The dc line can be loaded upto thermal limit of the line or converter equipment.

3. **Short circuit current** : The interconnection of two ac systems by an ac line increases the short circuit current in both the systems. This may require replacement of existing circuit breakers. However, the interconnection of ac systems by a dc line does not increase the short circuit current to a large extent and it is limited automatically by the grid/gate control of the converters to rated current of the dc line.

4. **Independent control of ac systems** : The ac systems interconnected by a dc line can be controlled independently. They can be completely independent as regards to frequency, system control, short circuit rating, future expansion etc.

5. **Fast change of energy flow** : The quick control of converter valves permit fast changes in magnitude and direction of energy flow when required. This results in increase in limits of transient stability, flexible coordination of system control at two ends, more economical use of power generation and reduction of system reserve and standby capacity.

6. **Lesser corona loss and radio interference** : The corona loss and radio interference is less in dc line as compared to ac line of same conductor diameter and voltage. Also in bad weather the corona and radio interference slightly decrease in case of dc line whereas they increase appreciably in case of ac line.

7. **Greater reliability** : A two conductor bipolar dc line is more reliable than a 3 conductor 3-phase line because in the event of a fault on one conductor, the other conductor of the dc line can continue to operate with ground return whereas 3-phase ac line can not operate on two phase. A monopolar dc line with ground return is simpler than a 3-phase ac line and equally reliable.

8. **Bulk power long distance transmission** : The dc line proves economical above a breakeven distance.

9. **No skin effect** : The skin effect is absent in dc line resulting in uniform current density in conductor and hence efficient utilization of conductor cross sectional area.

10. **No charging current** : Continuous line charging currents are absent in HVDC overhead lines and cables.
11. **No compensation required** : No series or shunt compensation is required even for long distance dc lines.
12. **Tower size and cost** : The phase to phase clearance and phase to ground clearance are smaller for dc transmission as compared to equivalent ac transmission lines for same power and distance. Also the load on the towers is lesser. Therefore the tower size is smaller and it is simple, easy to install and cheaper. Also the right-of-way cost is less.
13. **No distance limit** : Practically there is no technical limit to the distance of power transmission in overhead line and in cable.
14. **Power factor** : Line power factor is always unity.
15. **Less cost** : A basic dc line is less costly compared with a three phase ac line because only two conductors are needed in dc line compared with three in ac line.
16. **Higher permissible voltage** : An ac line has to be insulated for peak value of the ac voltage wave while useful value is only the rms value. Therefore, for the same insulation an increased transmission voltage can be adopted in the case of dc transmission. In case of cables the natural dielectric strength of insulation is substantially greater (over 3 times) in dc than in ac. As a result the working voltage of a dc cable can be as much as 5 times its ac working voltage.
17. **Longer life of cables** : Phenomena of dielectric fatigue is absent in dc so that the insulation has longer life.
18. **Increased transmission capacity** : For the same percentage loss a double circuit 3-phase ac line can transmit double power if converted to a 3-pole dc line. A single EHV cable can transmit 3 times power on dc as compared to on ac due to increased working stress, elimination of dielectric losses, absence of skin and proximity effects, elimination of eddy current losses etc.
19. **Ground return** : Ground can be used as a return conductor in the case of dc systems.

7.3 DISADVANTAGES OF HVDC TRANSMISSION

Apart from many advantages the HVDC transmission has a few disadvantages too. These are :

1. **Expensive converters :** The converters required at both the ends of a line have proved to be reliable but expensive. Therefore HVDC can be used economically only for long distance transmission.
2. **Reactive power requirement :** The operation of the converters at the ends of line require supply of reactive power from the ac system which may be as large as 75% of the active power. Hence the ac systems should be capable of supplying the reactive power.
3. **Harmonics and filters :** The converters produce lot of harmonics both in dc and ac sides which may cause interference with communication lines. Filters are required on the ac side of each converter for reducing the magnitude of harmonics in the ac network. These increase cost of the converter station.
4. **No reactive power can be transmitted :** Reactive power can not be transmitted over the HVDC line and therefore reactive power demand of ac systems at the two ends should be met themselves independently.
5. **Less overload capacity :** The converters have very little overload capacity and hence should be operated carefully within the limit.
6. **Absence of transforming equipment :** There is no equipment to transform voltages in dc and hence all transformation is to be done on the ac side.
7. **Absence of suitable circuit breaker :** In ac there is natural zero in current waveform every half cycle which facilitates circuit breaking. In dc the absence of natural zero in the current creates problem for circuit breaking. HVDC system does not have suitable HVDC circuit breakers.
8. **Complex control :** Control of HVDC substations and transmission is very complex.
9. **Losses and cooling system :** HVDC substations have additional losses in converter valves (thyristors) for which a suitable cooling system is necessary to dissipate the heat.

7.4 CONVERTER STATION EQUIPMENT

A schematic diagram of a typical HVDC converter station is shown in Fig. 7.4.

A HVDC converter station has 3-phase ac bus, ac circuit breakers, transformers, converter valves (thyristors), ac filters, shunt capacitors, smoothing reactors, dc filters etc. The transformers of the station are also called as converter transformers. The converter valves may convert ac to dc or dc to ac *i.e.*, they

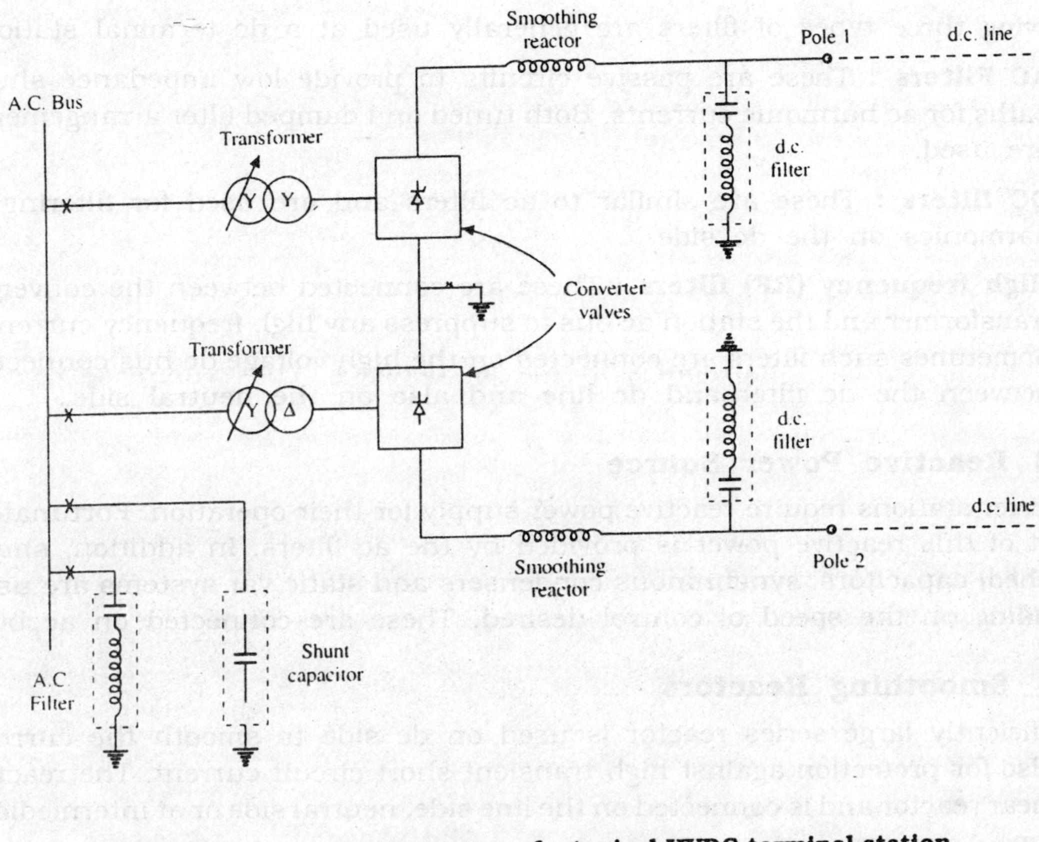

Fig. 7.4 : Schematic diagram of a typical HVDC terminal station

act as rectifier as well as inverter depending upon the requirement. A brief description of the equipments at the converter station is given in following sections.

7.4.1 Converter Transformers

The converter transformers are connected between ac bus and converter valves. The converter transformers can have different configurations depending upon the circuit chosen. The leakage reactance of the transformer is chosen to limit the short circuit current through any valve. DC magnetization of the transformer core may occur due to unequal firing of valves. The transformers are specially designed to withstand dc voltage stress and increased eddy current losses due to harmonic currents. They are also provided with suitable tap changers.

7.4.2 Filters

Following three types of filters are generally used at a dc terminal station :

1. **AC Filters** : These are passive circuits to provide low impedance shunt paths for ac harmonic currents. Both tuned and damped filter arrangements are used.
2. **DC filters** : These are similar to ac filters and are used for filtering of harmonics on the dc side.
3. **High frequency (RF) filters** : These are connected between the converter transformer and the station ac bus to suppress any high frequency currents. Sometimes such filters are connected on the high voltage dc bus connected between the dc filter and dc line and also on the neutral side.

7.4.3 Reactive Power Source

Converter stations require reactive power supply for their operation. Fortunately a part of this reactive power is provided by the ac filters. In addition, shunt (switched) capacitors, synchronous condensers and static var systems are used depending on the speed of control desired. These are connected on ac bus.

7.4.4 Smoothing Reactors

A sufficiently large series reactor is used on dc side to smooth the current and also for protection against high transient short circuit current. The reactor is a linear reactor and is connected on the line side, neutral side or at intermediate location.

7.4.5 DC Switchgear

This is usually a modified ac equipment used to interrupt small dc currents (employed as disconnecting switches). The dc breakers or metallic return transfer breakers are used if required for interruption of rated dc load currents.

In addition to above equipments, ac switchgear and associated equipment for protection and measurement are also part of the converter station.

7.5 GROUND RETURN

The monopolar and homopolar dc links usually use ground as return path of the current. The ground path has a low resistance and, therefore, low power loss as compared to a metallic conductor path provided the ground electrodes are properly designed. The ground return refers to the return path for currents through the ground or sea or both.

The cost of a monopolar or homopolar link with ground return is much less than the cost of such a link with metallic return conductor. In a bipolar link the main advantage of providing ground return is that the line can be built in stages. Initially the power capability requirement is generally less and the dc line can be set up as a monopolar link with ground return. When the load requirement increases the second line can be set up to complete the bipolar link. Thus a considerable part of the investment can be deferred to the next stage. In the event of one of the lines of bipolar link under repair or maintenance or fault, the link can be operated as monopolar link with ground return thus increasing reliability of the system.

Ground return has many problems. The main problems are :

1. design of grounding electrodes for low cost of installation and maintenance.
2. location and screening of electrodes so that ground currents cause negligible corrosion of buried and immersed metallic structures such as water pipelines.
3. prevention of interference caused by ground currents with other services.
4. control of surface gradients near the electrode for safety of persons, live stock and fish.

7.6 APPLICATIONS

The application of HVDC transmission may be of the following types. In practice, combination of the types of application may exist :

1. Power transmission over long overhead lines.
2. Power transmission through underground or submarine cables.
3. Interconnection of individually controlled AC systems.
4. AC and DC lines in parallel.
5. DC transmission and AC distribution.
6. Interconnection of different frequency AC systems.

These are explained in following sections.

7.6.1 Power Transmission over long Overhead Lines

Power transmission over long overhead lines is used to transmit large blocks of relatively cheap power from remote sources to load centres situated far away from the generating stations. The cost of dc transmission line is less than that of an ac line while the cost of the terminal stations in case of dc is high. In case of long distance transmission lines, the total cost becomes smaller for HVDC transmission.

7.6.2 Power Transmission through Underground or Submarine Cables

In some cases the interconnecting link between ac systems has to use submarine or underground cables. Cable transmission with ac is not possible for a distance of more than 50 kms due to the problem of charging currents. For longer distances HVDC is the only solution. Sometimes power transmission in congested urban areas has to be done through underground cables for which only HVDC is feasible.

7.6.3 Interconnection of Individually Controlled AC Systems

HVDC transmission can be used for interconnecting two ac systems controlled individually and may be operating at slightly different frequencies *i.e.*, asynchronously. In these cases the dc line may have zero or negligible length. A dc link with zero line length is called as back to back dc link.

7.6.4 AC and DC lines in Parallel

It is possible to transmit a part of the power by interconnection with a dc link while the rest of the power is transmitted over an ac line. The dc link can be used with the advantage for control of power flow.

7.6.5 DC Transmission and AC Distribution

The high voltage ac system can be connected to a distribution system or secondary transmission system through a relatively short dc link. The main advantage of dc link is ease of control of power flow and a reduced short circuit current.

7.6.6 Interconnection of Different Frequency AC Systems

When it is necessary to interconnect two power systems having different frequencies e.g. 50 Hz and 60 Hz systems, the HVDC system is very suitable. The dc link has technical advantages so that the system can be interconnected even with the dc line of zero length. Such a dc link with zero line length is also called as back to back dc link.

REVIEW QUESTIONS

7.1 Why is negative polarity of overhead conductor preferred in HVDC systems?

7.2 What types of dc links are used in present day power systems? Explain each of them with neat diagrams.

7.3 Discuss the advantages of HVDC transmission.

7.4 Discuss the disadvantages of HVDC transmission.

7.5 Describe the various equipments used in a converter station of HVDC systems.

7.6 What is ground return? Why is it used? What are the problems associated with the use of ground as the return conductor?

7.7 Discuss the applications of HVDC transmission.